Also available at all good book stores

9781785317927

9781801500630

9781801500067

9781801500937

9781801501149

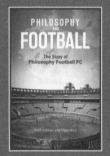

9781801500999

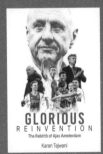

9781801500692

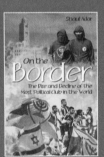

9781801500951

9781801500739

QARABAG

EMANUELE GIULIANELLI

QARABAG

THE TEAM WITHOUT A CITY
and Their Quest to Conquer Europe

First published in Italy. *Qarabag: La squadra senza città alla conquista dell'Europa*, Ultra, 2018

This edition published by Pitch Publishing, 2022

Pitch Publishing
9 Donnington Park,
85 Birdham Road,
Chichester,
West Sussex,
PO20 7AJ

www.pitchpublishing.co.uk
info@pitchpublishing.co.uk

A CIP catalogue record is available for this book
from the British Library.

ISBN 978 1 80150 092 0

Typesetting and origination by Pitch Publishing
Printed and bound in India by Replika Press Pvt. Ltd.

Contents

Dedicated to Veronica

Transliteration

MOST OF the names of the people and places that appear in this book are in the Azerbaijani language, which uses a script with characters and sounds that differ greatly from the Latin script used in English.

I have employed the international transcription criteria for transliteration, attempting to write everything in the form used most commonly in texts written in English and by leading press organisations in the English-speaking world.

What complicates this is that many words have multiple transliterations rather than a single equivalent. One example is provided by the place name Agdam; in the original spelling it is written Ağdam, while western transliterations use both Aghdam and Agdam, the version you will find in this book.

Hours could be spent discussing the word that gives this book its title: Qarabag. The disputed region between Armenia and Azerbaijan is called Qarabağ in the Azerbaijani language. Over the decades, the name has been westernised in a variety of ways: Qarabagh (as it appears in the club's official website address), Qarabag,

Karabakh, Karabagh and even Garabagh. The form you will find in the pages that follow is the same as the one on the cover.

One final note on the terms used in this book. I have used 'Azerbaijani' rather than 'Azeri' almost exclusively. 'Azeri' often refers to ethnic Azerbaijani populations living in Iran, while in English the terms are equivalent, according to the most commonly used dictionaries.

1

Qarabag is Agdam

AGDAM NO longer exists.

Rubbed out by the war, razed to the ground by the hatred and blind fury of boorish nationalism, of flag waving, flags later used as shrouds to cover coffins and corpses. I will not linger here to explain how war in general has no meaning other than for those who foment it and feed off blood and the dead; I will instead try, as best I can, not to take the side of either of the contenders in a territorial dispute that has turned into a fratricidal bloodbath, a storm of hatred, an insane and irrational yearning for destruction.

What I will try to do is tell a story, to talk about what has happened and what is happening, with some attempt to speculate on what will or what may happen. Or what can never happen. I will not lose my way in controversy. I will not try to say who is right and who is wrong because in a conflict between neighbours in which some 1,500 to 2,300 civilians and some 25,000 to 36,000 soldiers have lost their lives, with a million refugees forced to leave their homes, in a war that has continued for years, for decades, all reason has been lost. The shadow of reason has vanished in the fine dust that rises from the rubble of Agdam; reason has lost control, stunned by the smell of blood emanating from the mangled bodies on the streets of Khojaly; and reason has shattered on the ground, breaking into a thousand pieces like the windowpanes at Ghazanchetsots Cathedral and Shusha Mosque.

The story I will tell is that of a football team, Qarabag Agdam FK, which has not played in its stadium, its city, since 12 May 1993. And that of the city, Agdam, Qarabag is now all that remains. Qarabag is Agdam.

2

Black garden, black gold

IN HIS book *Azerbaijan Diary*, the American journalist Thomas Goltz tells the extraordinary story of how he found himself, almost by chance, an eyewitness on the front line during the war centred on the area of the South Caucasus commonly known as Nagorno-Karabakh. He sets out by questioning the very name of the former Soviet region, 'The Soviet/Russian designation for Karabakh lives on in press and scholarly reports that use "Nagorno-Karabakh" or even via the acronym "NKAO", which translates to the "Autonomous Territory of Mountainous Karabakh". Both uses are ridiculous, because there is a perfectly good word in English to replace the Russian adjective Nagorno, namely "Mountainous".'

Yet the denomination Nagorno-Karabakh embodies all the complexity, cultural richness and contradictions of a region in which the word 'peace' disappeared from the vocabulary 30 years ago. While Nagorno, as explained by Goltz, is a Russian adjective that translates as 'mountainous', the name Karabakh, the traditional pre-Soviet toponym for the region, is in turn made up of two words of different origin: kara, meaning 'black', and bakh, meaning 'garden', a term from the Farsi language, Persian. To make the mixture even richer and the tangle increasingly inextricable, the local Armenian population uses the term Artsakh to describe this rocky and harsh patch of land, wedged between Armenia and Azerbaijan and disputed by the two countries for decades.

In this whole affair, as in every dispute involving the Caucasus, words are not just important, they are crucial; they too become a battle ground and pretext for clashes that are not merely verbal in nature. As young teenagers we are taught at school that the same object varies in weight depending on which planet we are carrying it on; in the history of relations between Armenia and Azerbaijan, words weigh the same as boulders, as bombs in the case of the Nagorno-Karabakh conflict. Words themselves become weapons, thrown on to the pile without any assessment of their explosive power: words such as genocide and ethnic cleansing. Words that become excuses for justifying massacres and destruction, words that are the pretext for razing towns and villages to the ground and forcing hundreds and thousands of people to leave their homes forever.

23 November 2017
Baku, Tortuga Pub, Terlan Aliyarbekov st., 9
A pool table in the middle of the room, background music so loud it makes communication between human beings barely possible: five people of different nationalities sitting at the same table, talking about football and

Nagorno-Karabakh the night after Qarabag Agdam FK's loss to Chelsea at the Baki Olimpyia Stadionu in a Champions League Group C game. Alongside me are the 63-year-old American war reporter, writer and director Thomas Goltz, who has granted us the honour of joining our happy band; his Azerbaijani chaperone Shakir Eminbeyli, journalist and cameraman; and Rustam Fataliyev, an Azerbaijani journalist currently working in the press office at Neftchi, known to some as Azerbaijan's answer to Juventus. Rustam was my kind and helpful guide during my stay in Baku; we had shared a friendship on Facebook for years without meeting in person. Also with us, our Dutch colleague Arthur Huizinga, who possesses an in-depth knowledge of all things Qarabag Agdam, about which he has written books of fundamental importance for anyone wanting to learn about the subject. He has shared many a memorable drink with me and Rustam, tasted local food and spent hours in endless discussions about the most absurd and unthinkable aspects of this wonderful game which, in the end, is only a pretext for talking about ourselves and our world: it is no coincidence that I once wrote a book of short stories entitled *Il calcio è un pretesto* (translated as *Football is a Pretext*).

George Michael belts out his 'Careless Whisper' over the speakers until Thomas asks the waiter to turn down the volume so we can talk and then orders a beer. The wave of sound produced by the clack of two pool balls breaks the monotony of the music, while the five of us no longer have to shout to make ourselves heard over the former Wham vocalist.

15

'What do you think about the Nagorno-Karabakh situation and the events in Agdam?' I ask Goltz.

The American stares at me with his icy eyes and begins to answer, starting from the premise I mentioned at the start of the chapter, but in harsher tones than those he uses in his book, 'I've never referred to it as Nagorno-Karabakh. I call it Mountainous Karabakh or Upper Karabakh. Nagorno is a Russian adjective that means mountainous. But all the refugees come from the valley: the term mystifies everything. Because if you refer to Karabakh as Nagorno, you start to wonder how there can be a valley and then where do all the refugees come from? This is one of the great Armenian victories: to dictate the terms we use to discuss the conflict.'

'I'd never thought about that aspect,' I tell him.

'Another great Armenian success is the word "enclave". Karabakh has never been an enclave. We have to be very specific. Often, we journalists are lazy and we take any cliché as valid: Karabakh becomes Nagorno and an enclave. But it isn't.'

Nagorno-Karabakh came into being as an Autonomous Oblast within the Azerbaijan Soviet Socialist Republic; therefore, despite being inhabited by a population with an Armenian majority, it cannot be considered an Armenian enclave since it is part of Azerbaijan.

Evgeny Vinokurov's text entitled *A Theory of Enclaves* from 2007 addresses the case of Karabakh, clearly explaining why he chose to include it in his list of enclaves:

'An opposite case is also possible if an enclave is still recognised de jure but has ceased to exist de facto. Such is the case with Nagorno-Karabakh and several small enclaves of Armenia in Azerbaijan and vice versa. The existence of such enclaves will be recognised, however, with the proviso that these enclaves do not function as such for all practical matters.

'There is at least one supplementary reason, in addition to formal international law, to include such enclaves in the scope of consideration. Their vulnerability may well cause the return of their enclave status at a later stage.'

At the end of the First World War, following the collapse of the Russian Empire, Armenia, Azerbaijan and Georgia, freed from previous occupation by Tsarist Russia, united to form the Transcaucasian Democratic Federative Republic (TDFR); this experiment of a union between the three different historically and culturally divided nations lasted no more than a few months. In May 1918, following the dissolution of the TDFR, Azerbaijan declared itself independent and founded the Azerbaijan Democratic Republic (ADR), the first Muslim parliamentary republic in history.

Tbilisi, 28 May 1918
The Azerbaijani National Council, consisting of Vice president Hasan-bey Agayev, Secretary Mustafa Mahmudov, Fatali Khan Khoyski, Khalil-bey Khas-Mammadov, Nasib-bey Usubbeyov, Mir Hidayat Seidov, Nariman-bey Narimanbeyov, Heybat-Gulu Mammadbeyov, Mehti-bey Hajinski, Ali Asker-bey Mahmudbeyov, Aslan-bey Gardashev, Sultan Majid Ganizadeh, Akber-Aga Sheykh-Ul-

Islamov, Mehdi-bey Hajibababeyov, Mammad Yusif Jafarov, Khudadad-bey Melik-Aslanov, Rahim-bey Vekilov, Hamid-bey Shahtahtinskiy, Fridun-bey Kocharlinski, Jamo-bey Hajinski, Shafi-bey Rustambeyov, Hosrov-Pashabey Sultanov, Jafar Akhundov, Mahammad Maherramov, Javad Melik-Yeganov and Haji Molla Akhund-zadeh adopts the following act of independence for Azerbaijan on 28 May 1918 in the city of Tiflis.

The political regime established in Russia during the Russian Revolution caused the collapse of various parts of the state structure and the abandonment of the Transcaucasus by Russian troops.

Left to their own devices, the Transcaucasian peoples took their destiny into their own hands and founded the Transcaucasian Democratic Federative Republic. However, in the subsequent political development, the Georgian people expressed their desire to separate from the Transcaucasian Democratic Federative Republic and create the Independent Georgian Democratic Republic.

Generated by the cessation of hostilities between Russia and the Ottoman Empire, the current political situation in Azerbaijan, and in particular the intolerable anarchy within the country, requires the need to create a separate state in Azerbaijan to free its people from the constraints that are the result of the current difficult internal and external situation. This state will consist of the Eastern and Southern Transcaucasus.

As a result, the National Council of Azerbaijan, established by an election, now declares to the nation:

1. Azerbaijan is henceforth a fully sovereign state; it consists of the southern and eastern parts of Transcaucasia under the authority of the Azerbaijani people.

2. It is resolved that the form of government of the independent Azerbaijani state is a democratic republic.

3. The Azerbaijani Democratic Republic is determined to establish friendly relations with all, especially with neighbouring nations and states.

4. The Azerbaijani Democratic Republic guarantees to all its citizens within its borders full civil and political rights, regardless of ethnic origin, religion, class, profession or sex.

5. The Azerbaijani Democratic Republic encourages the free development of all nationalities inhabiting its territory.

6. Until the Azerbaijani Constituent Assembly is convened, the supreme authority over Azerbaijan is vested in a universally elected National Council and the provisional government responsible to this council.

Although little known, the short-lived story of the ADR represented a milestone, a real watershed for the government of a state populated by an Islamic majority. Its legislation, as made clear by point four of the Declaration of Independence, guaranteed the equality of all citizens and provided for universal suffrage, also guaranteeing the right to vote to women with a law approved by parliament on 21 July 1919, before the United States of America and many western democracies.

The first disputes over Nagorno-Karabakh – between the Azerbaijani Democratic Republic and the so-called First Republic of Armenia – date from this time. This also followed the struggle for control of Baku, Azerbaijan's current capital; the city remained outside the ADR since it was under the control firstly of the Armenian armed forces, who established the so-called Baku Commune, the Ottomans and, finally, the British Army, who aimed to take full charge of the wells in the city on the shores of the Caspian Sea. The date of the birth of the global oil industry conventionally coincides with the first gush and extraction of oil in industrial quantities from wells dug by specialist machinery in Bibiheybat and Balakhany, on the southern outskirts of Baku, between 1847 and 1848; this predates the first American borehole at Titusville, Pennsylvania, by more than a decade. By 1899, the area around Azerbaijan's modern-day capital was the first in the world to produce and refine the so-called black gold. But the Caucasian nation was also a leader in offshore oil extraction: the first exploitation of a marine oil well, located about 30 metres from the shore of the south bay of Baku, was also in Bibiheybat. The first industrial technique for the distillation of kerosene was developed in Baku and the first oil refining plant was built in the city in 1859.

In the late 19th and early 20th centuries, Baku represented for the oil industry what the area around the Klondike River, in north-western Canada, represented for the gold rush. A maritime city, contested for decades between Persia and Russia – to whose dominion it was definitively ceded by means of the agreements of 1806, 1813 and 1828 – it found itself at the centre of attention for the entire European continent, for all the nations that glimpsed the enormous potential of the black gold and the importance of being the first to gain control and exploitation of the Caspian Sea deposits. By 1905, Baku was already producing 50 per cent of the world's oil and extremely wealthy oil magnates began building luxury residences outside the walls of the Old City, which was increasingly losing its central role as a result. The great opulence of the oil companies was offset by the conditions of extreme poverty in which the industry's workers were forced to live. The divisions, however, were not only between industrialists and workers, between entrepreneurs and labourers. A sinister rift in the social fabric was getting wider and wider, in the words of the American journalist and writer Steve LeVine, 'The hate-filled ethnic divide that roiled the local Azerbaijani Turk and Armenian populations. The Armenians were, to a large degree, members of the wealthy establishment of industrialists, merchants, and managers and later, the local leadership of Lenin's Bolshevik revolutionaries. The native Azeris, often far less educated, filled many of the jobs in the oilfields, rail road yards, and factories.'

This discontent created a breeding ground for revolutionary ideas that publicly manifested themselves in the general strike of 1904, in the wake of which workers on the Baku oilfields succeeded in negotiating the first-ever contract between workers and managers in Russian history. The agreements reached in the oil sector did not serve to calm the situation in an ever more tumultuous region, increasingly the target of international interests and groups looking to stir up rebellions or create instability. From that moment on, the history of the city and of Azerbaijan as a whole would be a succession of tensions, violence and wars. A key player in events that took place in Baku during those years was none other than a young Joseph Stalin who, in February 1905, witnessed a wave of ethnic violence between Armenians and Azeris that led to the deaths of at least 2,000 people.

When the three republics of Armenia, Azerbaijan and Georgia created the TDFR in 1918, the city of Baku was left out, as already mentioned: to support the city's separate position with regard to the fledgeling geopolitical experiment in the South Caucasus, a British military contingent arrived secretly by sea from Iran, coming, in fact, to occupy Baku and secure British investments, defending the oilfields against Turkish attacks. But things did not go according to George V's plans. Turkish and Azeri troops bombed the city, while the unprepared British soldiers retreated by sea under cover of darkness. At the end of the First World War, the Turks were also forced to evacuate the city: Baku thus became the capital of an independent Azerbaijan, of the Azerbaijani Democratic Republic for almost two years. But on 20 April 1920, the Red Army marched on Baku, putting an end to any British ambitions in the region – with George V hoping for a crown mandate in the Caucasus in 1919. This also marked the end of a wonderful example of democracy in the Muslim world, of a system that was ahead of its time even compared to many western countries, and the beginning of a dominion that would last until the late 1980s and the collapse of the Soviet Union. The colours used for the first time on the flag of the Azerbaijani Democratic Republic in 1918 have been taken up by the Republic of Azerbaijan, independent since 1991, which has made them its own. The constitution of November 1995 establishes the following with Article 23:,

> The state flag of the Republic of Azerbaijan will consist of three horizontal stripes of the same width. The upper stripe must be blue; the central stripe must be red; and the lower stripe must be green. There must be a white half-moon and an eight-pointed star in the middle of the red stripe on both sides of the flag. The proportion of width to length must be 1 to 2.

The Transcaucasus experiment and the short-lived independence of Armenia, Azerbaijan and Georgia failed to stop the ethnic violence and massacres; 31 March 1918 saw the start in Baku of the so-called 'March Days', with the massacre of 12,000 Azerbaijanis by Armenian-supported Bolsheviks, as reported by the *New York Times* (most likely citing Azerbaijani officials). On 28 May 1918,

Armenia and Azerbaijan declared their independence and on 15 September, the Ottoman Army entered the city and condoned revenge on the Azerbaijanis, who massacred non-Muslims; an estimated 10,000 to 30,000 Armenians were brutally killed.

In January 1919, the Governorate General of Karabakh was created inside the Azerbaijani Democratic Republic; it was also at this time that the name I have already discussed at length, Nagorno-Karabakh, was coined by Dashnak, the Armenian Revolutionary Federation, the party that led the Baku Commune, later banned from political life following the occupation of the Caucasus republics by the Soviet Union. The violence continued, as did the political upheaval in a region that was increasingly becoming a hot potato in the hands of Stalin, who was preparing to become general secretary of the Communist Party of the Soviet Union (CPSU). Between 1918 and 1922, the future Soviet leader would, in fact, hold the role of people's commissar of nationalities (Narkomnats) within the government; its peculiarities were the questions that concerned all non-Russian populations within the Soviet republics, with related issues linked to ethnic groups and territorial disputes. The Armenian Soviet Socialist Republic continued to exert claims over the Karabakh territories belonging to the Azerbaijan Soviet Socialist Republic.

In a telegram to Ordzhonikidze on 8 July 1920, Stalin clearly expressed his opinion on the territorial conflicts between Armenia and Azerbaijan, focused on Karabakh, for the first time, 'My opinion is that it is impossible to manoeuvre endlessly between the parties. It is necessary to support one of the two parties, in this case Azerbaijan and Turkey. I have spoken to Lenin and he failed to show any interest.'

On 5 July 1921, the Kavbiuro, the Caucasian Politburo of the Central Committee of Russian Communists (Bolsheviks), decided:

> Taking into consideration the need for a national peace between Muslims and Armenians, the importance of economic relations between Upper and Lower Karabakh and ongoing relations between Upper Karabakh and Azerbaijan, Nagorno-Karabakh will be kept within the borders of the Azerbaijan Soviet Socialist Republic and extensive autonomy will be given to Nagorno-Karabakh with the city of Shusha as its administrative centre.

The Union of Soviet Socialist Republics was officially founded on 30 December 1922 and the Nagorno-Karabakh Autonomous Oblast (abbreviated as NKAO) was created within the Azerbaijan Soviet Socialist Republic (SSR) on 7 July 1923. The first point in the constitution of the NKAO from the Central Executive Committee of Soviet Azerbaijan reads:

> Establishing an autonomous oblast on the Armenian side of Nagorno-Karabakh, as a constituent part of the Azerbaijan Soviet Socialist Republic, with its capital in Khankendi.

Whether this decision should have been made is up for debate, but Stalin did in fact decide to incorporate the Karabakh region, whose population was mostly Armenian, into the Azerbaijan SSR. Not only was it decided that the NKAO territories would be assigned to Azerbaijan, not Armenia, the expression of the Stalinist policy of divide and rule, the decision also took on strategic importance on the great chessboard of international alliances. Lenin and Stalin were well aware that the fledgeling Soviet Russia was not militarily strong and needed an ally to provide it with support in the event of aggression by allied powers attempting to take advantage of an unstable political situation following the revolution and civil war. The two Soviet leaders, therefore, considered it a necessary sacrifice to cede the lands claimed by Armenia to the Azerbaijan SSR in exchange for military aid from Mustafa Kemal Atatürk; the supplies of gold and Russian arms to the Turkish National Movement, which allowed the Kemalists to take power in Turkey after the defeat of the Ottoman Empire and to successfully conclude the Armenian campaign (1920) and Greco-Turkish War (1919–1922), should also be seen in this light.

The key moment that sealed this alliance and indelibly marked the destiny of Nagorno-Karabakh, determining the events of successive decades, was the Treaty of Moscow of 16 March 1921 – later reaffirmed by the Treaty of Kars on 13 October of the same year – in which the borders of Turkey and the Caucasian republics of Armenia, Azerbaijan and Georgia were established, according to the agreements already examined in detail.

Moscow, 23 December 1947
Council of Ministers of the Soviet Union

The Council of Ministers of the Armenian
SSR is allowed to use the buildings and homes
vacated by the Azerbaijani population as a result
of their resettlement on the Kura-Aras plain in
the Azerbaijan SSR for the settlement of foreign
Armenians arriving in the Armenian SSR.

Homes vacated as a result of their resettlement. Words
whitewashed like tombs. An ascetic language, as cold as
it is clean, to name a very different and terrible reality:
deportation.

Thousands of Azerbaijanis living inside the Armenian
SSR were forced to leave their homes and land to make
way for Armenians from the diaspora, called from
abroad to live on Armenian SSR land. The Stalinist
strategy was simple. Relations with Turkey had soured,
especially following the rejection of the Soviet request
for joint control of the Black Sea Straits and territorial
claims by the USSR over the Turkish territories of Kars
and Ardahan.

Turkey was becoming a most uncomfortable neighbour
for the Soviet Union, and Armenia, therefore, took on
fundamental strategic importance as the region that
served as a border between the two powers. As a result,
Stalin decided to free the Armenian SSR of its component
of Azerbaijanis and to invite Armenians from abroad to
populate the vacated areas, with a view to strengthening
the SSR and freeing the dominant ethnic group from
the distractions of intra-ethnic clashes. An Armenia

free of Muslims became a real Soviet stronghold against the new Turkish enemy. That was not all: Stalin also feared that, in the event of an armed conflict, Azerbaijan and its population might become a sort of Turkish fifth column, an enemy at home against which they would have to defend themselves, given the feeling of brotherhood between the two peoples.

However, the table below shows the evolution of the demographic composition of the population of the Autonomous Oblast of Nagorno-Karabakh, from 1939 to 1979, according to data taken from the ninth five-year plan for Nagorno-Karabakh:

Population Nagorno Karabak	1939		1959		1970		1979	
	absolute	per cent	absolute	per cent	absolute	per cent	absolute	per cent
Total	150.8	100.0	130.4	100.0	150.3	100.0	162.2	100.0
Armenians	132.8	88.1	110.1	84.8	121.1	80.5	123.1	75.9
Azerbaijani	14.1	9.4	18.0	13.8	27.2	18.1	37.3	23.0
Russians	3.2	2.1	1.8	1.4	1.3	0.9	1.3	0.8

When Nikita Khrushchev took over at the Kremlin in 1956, instigating a policy of détente, there followed a period of relative calm in the clashes between Armenians and Azerbaijanis, despite the ongoing discontent and frustration on the part of the Armenians of Nagorno-Karabakh, who still felt they were being forced to be part of a republic to which they did not belong.

In 1977, the new Constitution of the Union of Soviet Socialist Republics, drawn up during the presidency of Leonid Brezhnev, confirmed what had already been known since 1923, in particular in Chapter 11 entitled 'The

Autonomous Region and the Autonomous Area'. In listing all the autonomous regions of the territory of the USSR, Article 87 states:

> The Azerbaijan Soviet Socialist Republic includes the Nagorno-Karabakh Autonomous Region.

The weight of this short sentence was not inconsiderable: the Armenians of Nagorno-Karabakh had once again begun to take steps towards secession at the end of Khrushchev's presidency, which became more intense during the drafting of the USSR's new fundamental charter. A crucial role in maintaining the status quo in the administration of the Autonomous Oblast of Nagorno-Karabakh was played by a key figure in the affairs of firstly Soviet, then independent Azerbaijan: Heydar Aliyev. Aliyev was born in 1923 in Nakhchivan, a region of the Azerbaijan SSR separated from the rest of the oblast, an enclave surrounded by Armenia which, like Nagorno-Karabakh, claimed ownership of it. The son of a railway worker, he began his political career between 1941 and 1944 in Baku in the ranks of the local Communist Party, eventually joining the Azeri People's Commissariat for Internal Affairs (NKGB). In 1967, he became head of the KGB in Azerbaijan and on 12 July 1969 was appointed first secretary of the Central Committee of Leonid Brezhnev's Communist Party of Azerbaijan, a position he held until 1982. In 1976, he became a candidate member of the Politburo of the Soviet Communist Party: his influential position, rise through the Soviet apparatus and President Brezhnev's esteem for him allowed Aliyev to have a say in the protection of the interests of the Azerbaijan SSR during the drafting of the new constitution.

According to the Soviet unitary constitutional document, the NKAO was represented by five deputies on the Supreme Soviet of the USSR's Soviet of Nationalities and 12 deputies on the Supreme Soviet of the Azerbaijan SSR.

3

Escalation

Stepanakert, 20 February 1988
Special meeting of the 20th session, the Soviet of People's
Deputies, Autonomous Oblast of Nagorno-Karabakh.

RESOLUTION:

Regarding the mediation for the transfer of
the Autonomous Oblast of Nagorno-Karabakh
from the Azerbaijan SSR to the Armenian SSR:

After repeatedly listening to and reviewing
the statements made by the people's deputies
of the Soviet Autonomous Oblast of Nagorno-
Karabakh 'regarding the mediation of the
Supreme Soviet SSR between the Azerbaijan
SSR and the Armenian SSR for the transfer of
the Autonomous Oblast of Nagorno-Karabakh
from the Azerbaijan SSR to the Armenian
SSR', the special session of the regional soviet of
the 20th regional soviet of Nagorno-Karabakh
resolved – acknowledging the requests made
by the workers of the Autonomous Oblast

of Nagorno-Karabakh – to ask the Supreme Soviets of the SSRs of Azerbaijan and Armenia to recognise the Armenian population of Nagorno-Karabakh's profound desire and to transfer the Autonomous Oblast of Nagorno-Karabakh from the Azerbaijan Soviet Socialist Republic to the Armenian SSR, while at the same time interceding with the Supreme Soviet of the USSR to reach a positive resolution on the transfer of the region from the Azerbaijan SSR to the Armenian SSR.

The die was cast. This was not the first formal request addressed to Moscow by the Armenian population of Karabakh for annexation to the Armenian SSR (the most important precedents dated from 1945, 1965 and 1977, the latter coming just after the drafting of the new constitution).

The request made in February 1988 was, however, to resound with a deafening echo in the corridors of Soviet power and among the people, in streets and in houses; it was also the fuse that lit a fire that would flare up in the region and has still to go out.

Hatred found its barbaric and brutal outlet in the days that followed the Nagorno-Karabakh regional soviet vote, in which the Azerbaijani deputies refused to take part. Demonstrations began in Yerevan, the capital of Armenia, in support of Armenian claims over Karabakh. Then war broke out.

* * *

'In February 1988, I was serving in the Soviet army in Russia's Ural region. When the conflict with the Armenians in Karabakh began, as soldiers we heard nothing about it. The Soviet government hid what was happening, from the military in particular. I only found out what was happening in June, when I returned home from military service. I found out that the Armenians had held their first demonstration in Khankendi on 13 February: they were calling for the unification of Karabakh with Armenia.

'On 21 February, the protest was held in Agdam and the demonstrators marched as far as Khankendi. In Askeran, between Khankendi and Agdam, the Soviet army and the Armenian police blocked the road, went over to the demonstrators and opened fire. Two people died; their names were Ali and Bakhtiyar. Many were wounded. This date marked the beginning of the conflict in Karabakh, which grew into a war as the years went on.'

These are the atrocious and specific words used by journalist and writer Vahid Qazi to tell me about the onset of hostilities in Karabakh. The names of the two young Azerbaijanis who died during the clashes, Ali Hajiyev and Bakhtiyar Guliyev, were revealed on Baku Radio by the deputy prosecutor-general of the Soviet Union, Aleksandr Katusev, who failed to specify, however, that one of the two victims had been killed by an Azerbaijani policeman. Katusev was reportedly reprimanded by his superiors for revealing the nationality of the two victims, but the reality was that by then the touchpaper had been lit and there were those who, consciously or unconsciously, were fanning the flames.

The events of Askeran and the first victims were swiftly followed by the pogroms of Sumgait, 30km from Baku. Groups of Azerbaijanis thirsty for revenge set out to kill Armenians and burn down their houses, one by one.

The situation was getting out of hand in an irreversible way and responses from the Kremlin were slow in coming. Despite the transparency and reforms, despite the *glasnost* and *perestroika*.

'In the name of our much oppressed population, we have the responsibility to warn respectfully the Peace Conference that all arbitrary solutions that would sacrifice the legitimate aspirations of Armenians [in Karabakh and Nakhchivan] would in the future become the source of new conflicts and perpetual convulsions.'

The text that the government of Armenia sent to the Paris peace conference on 15 May 1919 – at which the victorious powers of the First World War were deciding the future geopolitical structures of Europe and the world as a whole – reread in the light of what happened in Sumgait and Nagorno-Karabakh, sounds more like a terrible prophecy than a warning.

* * *

PLAY IN ONE ACT[1]
DRAMATIS PERSONAE

Dmitry Yazov: defence minister of the Soviet Union

---

1   The drama was created by the author, based on what was reported on the book by Thomas de Waal, *Black Garden, Armenia and Azerbaijan Through Peace and War* (New York University Press, 2003)

Mikhail Sergeyevich Gorbachev: general secretary of the Communist Party of the Soviet Union

Viktor Vlasov: interior minister of the Soviet Union

Eduard Shevardnadze: foreign affairs minister of the Soviet Union

Aleksandr Vladimirovich Yakovlev: Gorbachev's advisor, president of the Glasnost Committee.

Scene: Moscow, Kremlin. It is 29 February 1988 and the Politburo is meeting to discuss the situation in the Caucasus and the developments following the Sumgait massacres.

YAZOV: But Mikhail Sergeyevich, in Sumgait we have to bring in, if you want – it may not be the word – but martial law.

GORBACHEV: A curfew.

YAZOV: We have to pursue this line firmly, Mikhail Sergeyevich, to stop it getting out of hand. We have to send in troops and restore order. After all, this is an isolated place and not Armenia with millions of people. Besides, that will surely have a sobering effect on others.

GORBACHEV: Aleksandr Vladimirovich and Dmitry Timofeyevich, you mean the possible situation in Baku, in Leninakan and in that town, where there is an Armenian area?

VLASOV: Kirovabad.

GORBACHEV: Kirovabad.

VLASOV: They smashed windows and that was all.

GORBACHEV: We have to bear in mind that they did not yet know what happened in Sumgait, but that this is growing like a snowball.

SHEVARNADZE: It is like a connecting vein. If in Armenia they find out about casualties, then it could cause trouble there.

YAKOVLEV: We must announce quickly that criminal cases have been opened in Sumgait and criminals have been arrested. We need that in order to cool passions. In Sumgait itself, the city newspaper should say this firmly and quickly.

GORBACHEV. The main thing now is we need to send the working class, people, people's volunteers into the fight with the criminals. That, I can tell you, will stop any hooligans and extremists. As happened in Alma-Ata. It's very important. Soldiers provoke hostility.

* * *

In reality, by now it was impossible to stop events unfolding; no one could have prevented the dormant hatred, held back for decades, from being released once the seal had been broken. All that remained was to pick up the pieces, because the monsters had already escaped. But then again, perhaps they were never entirely inside the perimeter made up of integration and tolerance in the first place. For one simple reason: the central state did not consider it necessary for these feelings to exist, for the peoples to live in harmony with each other. The USSR in the late 1980s was nothing more than the result of Stalin's modelling; a boundless empire consisting of a puzzle of peoples and nations, whose pieces could be moved and mixed at will, depending on the opportunity at that particular moment.

The book *On My Country and the World*[2] states that: 'Borders were carved out arbitrarily, the rights of one or other nationality were flagrantly violated, and during and immediately after World War II many nationalities were subjected to wholesale repression. They were deported from their ancient homelands and resettled in remote parts of the country. Tens of thousands of these people perished in the process.'

The events of Sumgait, during which it is estimated that 32 people lost their lives – without needing to distinguish between how many were Armenians and how many were Azeris – marked a watershed in the events of Nagorno-Karabakh, a point of no return. It was clear from that moment on that settling the dispute peacefully would no longer be an option.

Two declarations swiftly followed each other, diametrically opposed in tone and meaning. On 15 June 1988, the Armenian Supreme Soviet voted to accept Nagorno-Karabakh into Armenia; the response was not slow in coming, because on 17 June the Azerbaijan Supreme Soviet reaffirmed that Nagorno-Karabakh remained part of Azerbaijan.

Moscow, 18 July 1988

The Presidium of the Supreme Soviet of the USSR, after examining the request of 15

---

2 Mikhail Gorbachev, *On My Country and the World* (Columbia University Press, New York, 2000)

June 1988 made by the Supreme Soviet of
the Republic of Armenia for the Autonomous
Oblast of Nagorno-Karabakh to be united with
Armenia, in conjunction with a request from the
Soviet of deputies of Nagorno-Karabakh, and
the decision of 17 June 1988 by the Supreme
Soviet of the Republic of Azerbaijan, according
to which it was unacceptable to make the
Autonomous Oblast of Nagorno-Karabakh part
of Armenia, considered changing the borders
and dividing Azerbaijan and Armenia on ethnic
and territorial grounds to be impossible on a
constitutional basis.

In issuing this verdict, the Presidium of the Supreme
Soviet of the USSR was guided by a provision of the
Constitution of the USSR (Article 78), according to
which the territory of the republic of the union cannot
be changed without its consent.

A decision to the contrary would contradict the
fundamental interests of the peoples of both republics and
cause serious damage to inter-ethnic relations in the area.

The Soviet Union – the Central State as Gorbachev
described it in his book – made the decision to maintain
the territorial status quo, being unable to remove a portion
of its territory from Azerbaijan without its consent.
However, the warning from the central authority was
severe. 'The authorities of Azerbaijan, Armenia and
the Autonomous Oblast of Nagorno-Karabakh,' the
document written by the Presidium of the Supreme Soviet
continued, 'have taken a superficial approach to assessing

the situation. They have failed to realise the political danger of unfounded requests to review the existing ethnic-territorial structure of the area and have adopted a passive attitude, assuming the position of waiting and watching.' Waiting and watching.

Between 18 and 20 September 1988, persecutions, raids and forced expulsions continued on both sides of the struggle. Armenians were expelled from Shusha, while Azerbaijanis were sent away from the city formerly known as Khankendi, which had taken the Armenian name of Stepanakert in honour of Stepan Shahumian, political leader and head of the Baku Commune. On 21 September, Moscow declared the introduction of martial law in Nagorno-Karabakh, while in November the Armenian leadership decided to undertake mass expulsions of Azerbaijanis from Armenia.

The waters were calmed for a few weeks between late 1988 and early 1989. On 7 December, during Gorbachev's visit to the United States and his meetings with outgoing president Ronald Reagan and the newly elected George Bush, the whole world was shaken by the terrible news of an earthquake that had struck the Soviet Caucasus.

The following day, the *New York Times* reported: 'One of the worst earthquakes in Soviet history left a wake of devastation along the Soviet-Turkish border Wednesday, with thousands reported dead in three southern Soviet republics.

'Foreign Minister Eduard A. Shevardnadze announced in New York that preliminary data indicated that thousands had been killed in the republics, Armenia, Georgia and Azerbaijan.

'"There's also been a lot of destruction," he said. He called the disaster "a terrible tragedy" for "all the people of the Soviet Union".

'The epicentre of the earthquake, which struck at 11:41 A.M. local time on Wednesday, was about 35 miles northwest of the city of Leninakan, the second-largest city in the Soviet Republic of Armenia, with a population of 225,000.

'Soviet television on Wednesday night showed film of vast destruction in two other centers in western Armenia. In the cities of Spitak and Kirovakan, buildings had been split in two and piles of apartment house rubble was topped by the twisted remnants of balconies.'

One of the most terrible disasters of the modern era had hit Armenia for the most part, as Azerbaijan and Georgia were only marginally affected. A quake of 6.8–6.9 on the Richter scale was focused on the north-western part of the Armenian SSR, with the epicentre located in the province of Lori, between the village of Nalband and the town of Spitak, which was razed to the ground completely in just 30 seconds. Estimates calculated the number of victims at between 25,000 and 50,000, concentrated mainly in the area between Spitak, Leninakan (now Gyumri) and Kirovakan (Vanadzor); the extensive damage and numerous deaths were caused, according to studies of the Armenian earthquake carried out by seismic engineers, by the poor quality of the construction materials used in many buildings, those dating in particular from the period of Leonid Brezhnev's presidency, described by Gorbachev as the 'Era of Stagnation'.

Gorbachev returned home and appealed, despite the Cold War, to all nations to help the USSR cope with a catastrophe of such magnitude and visited the areas of Armenia hit by the earthquake in person between 10 and 11 December.

International solidarity was surprising; the whole world joined efforts to support devastated Armenia and Gorbachev's Soviet Union. One of the most memorable projects was Rock Aid Armenia, which saw international music stars such as Led Zeppelin, Genesis, Iron Maiden, Bon Jovi and Pink Floyd raise funds to support the population and reconstruction of the areas affected by the cataclysm.

But even a tragedy such as the Armenian earthquake became a political pretext to quell the uprising in Karabakh, to conceal from the eyes of the world, focused on the Caucasus because of events in Spitak, the massacres and ethnic cleansing taking place. The months immediately preceding the tragedy had seen the founding of the Karabakh Committee, formed by a group of Armenian intellectuals, among whom the name of Levon Ter-Petrosyan stood out. Immediately perceived by the population as the nation's de facto political leaders, the committee pursued the goal of unifying Nagorno-Karabakh with Armenia. On 11 December 1988, during Gorbachev's visit to the areas affected by the earthquake, taking advantage of the general confusion in the region, the Soviet authorities arrested the members of the Karabakh Committee, accused of obstructing the arrival of international humanitarian aid from Azerbaijan. In reality, the central government feared an anti-communist opposition movement that risked, by bringing into play the question of reviewing the Azerbaijan and Armenian SSR border, undermining the central authority of Moscow and questioning presidential control, as well as that of the Supreme Soviet, over the entire territory of the Soviet Union.

The events that took place in Karabakh in the late 1980s were nothing more than the final shove against a colossus with feet of clay, an increasingly weak USSR that would fall, broken into a thousand pieces, shortly afterwards. Disarmed by the blows of perestroika, a victim of the same contradictions and choices that failed to take into account the legitimate aspirations of the people that made it up and, more generally, of single citizens, seen only as a shapeless mass, as a collective and not as individuals.

4

Imaret

Time has plunged me into an ocean of pain and woe,
Parted me with my sun-faced; all is dark wherever I go.

My patience has reached its limit, O God Almighty
on high!
Either allow me to join him, or have mercy and let me die.

In vain I implored and begged you, you left and never
returned.
Now come and look at me, sun-faced, see into what I
have turned.

How long must I pine in longing – my life is all misery.
Have pity, at least for a moment; beloved, remember me.

What terrible tortures I suffer! Our parting I cannot bear.
Am I worthy of nothing better than eternal grief and
despair?

Our parting has stolen my reason, my soul has
   forgotten repose.
Behold how merciless fortune has doomed me to
   endless woes.

I wonder why my cruel lover will not have pity on me.
I burn in the flame of parting – the one who lit it was he!

How beautiful were those days when I was together
   with you.
Now I am broken-hearted, sadly my fate I rue.

For a while I was reunited with my lover, that pitiless man.
But now I am once again lonely – I have become Natavan.

Translated by Dorian Rottenberg

Natavan – powerless. A play on words. These lines were
written by Khurshidbanu Natavan, considered one of the
greatest poets in the history of Azerbaijan. Born in the
walled city of Shusha on 6 August 1832, Natavan, whose
full name was Khurshidbanu Natavan Mehti Quli Khan
Qizi, was the daughter of Mehdigulu Khan Javanshir, the
last khan of the Karabakh Khanate. The Javanshir dynasty
reigned over the semi-independent Turkish khanate of
Karabakh – placed under Iranian sovereignty from its
establishment in 1750 until its absorption into the Russian
Empire in 1822, when it became part of the Elisabethpol
Governorate – now known as Ganja, in Azerbaijan.

The precursor of the khanate was the province of
Karabakh in the Safavid Empire, ruled from 1501 by

a dynasty with a Turkish language and culture that originated in Persian Kurdistan. On the death of the Shah of Persia, Nader Shah Afshar, in Quchan in 1747, the empire's territory was divided into several khanates with varying levels of autonomy. Panah Ali Khan Javanshir took advantage of the situation and ruled his khanate as a kingdom independent from Persian rule. The representative of the Javanshir dynasty also subjected the five Armenian principalities of Gyulistan, Jaraberd, Khachen, Varand and Dizaq to his rule, thanks above all to the help of Prince Melik Shahnazar II Shahnazarian of Varand, who was the first to accept their sovereignty.

After the death of her father in 1845, Natavan, who had also studied in Tbilisi alongside the Russian aristocracy, began writing ghazals and rubaiyats composed in the Persian and Azerbaijani languages; her first works date from the 1850s.

In 1850, she married an aristocrat from Dagestan, Khasay Khan Usmiyev – who held the rank of *Komdiv* (Commanding Officer of the Division) in the Red Army – although theirs was not a love story. Natavan was forced to move to Tbilisi for more than two years due to her husband's business, and her experience in what is now the Georgian capital helped the poet broaden her outlook on the world and had a profound influence on her ideas and thought. In 1858, during a stay in Baku in the house of the judge Piguliyevski, she met the famous writer Alexandre Dumas, who became close friends with her husband Khasay Khan. In his book *Adventures in the Caucasus*, Dumas recalls with great respect the family of the poet from Karabakh, who separated from Khasay Khan in

1860, when she refused to follow him to Dagestan and instead chose to stay in Shusha. Her Shusha.

The daughter of the last khan was profoundly committed to the growth of the city and the region as a whole, engaging in a variety of philanthropic activities and works; one of the poet's best-known projects for the benefit of the people of Karabakh was the laying of a pipeline to bring water to the city of Shusha – capital of the land over which her father had reigned – for the first time, in 1883. The Russian daily newspaper *Kavkaz* wrote that Natavan, taking into account everything she was doing for her city and its people, 'has left an eternal mark in the memories of the inhabitants of Shusha and her glory will be passed down from generation to generation'. In 1885, following the tragic and untimely death of her beloved son Abbas, Khurshidbanu decided to assume the name Natavan, meaning 'powerless'.

One of the many merits for which Natavan should be recognised in assisting the growth of her homeland is undoubtedly the development and popularity of the famous Karabakh horse breed. Her stables were accepted as the best in all of Azerbaijan. During an international competition in Paris in 1867, a Karabakh horse from the poet's stables in Shusha, with the unequivocal name of Khan, won a silver medal; at another event two years later, in which horses representing every region of the Russian Empire were competing, Karabakh horses from the Natavan stables won several awards: Meymun secured a silver medal and Tokmak a bronze, while the third stallion, Alyetmez, won a title and was chosen as a breeding stallion for the Emperor of Russia's stables.

The website www.karabakh.org explains more:

'The stud farm in Agdam, which existed until 1991, would send a contingent of between 20 and 25 horses to Moscow every year for export to western countries.

'The Karabakh is a mesomorphic horse, with a height of between 14.1 and 15.2 hands. It has a medium long neck and a short and robust back with a rounded rump. Its limbs are lean and joints well defined and particularly solid. Its hooves are extremely hard. It is marked at the height of the saddle: on the right, with the last two digits of its year of birth; on the left, with the registration number of the foal in the corresponding year.

'Karabakhs are one of the few breeds to have been bred exclusively as saddle horses in the former Soviet Union.

'The fact that specimens of the breed were given as official gifts to historical figures provides an indication of their popularity. They were ridden by the sons of the tsar and top generals alike. Pushkin himself praised the courage of his Karabakh and, in 1956, First Secretary Khrushchev gave a stallion as a gift to Queen Elizabeth II.'

Khan Gizi – the khan's daughter, as she was then known among her people – died in Shusha on 2 October 1897. As a sign of esteem and gratitude, the citizens carried her coffin on their shoulders in a procession to the city of Agdam, about 30km north-west of Shusha, for burial in the family tomb in an area known as Imaret.

In the 17th century, Imaret was one of the racecourses attended by the khans of Karabakh. As the centuries passed, a significant portion of the area became the family tomb of the rulers of Karabakh. Buried there, among others, were Panah Ali Khan, Mehr Ali Bcy and

Mahdiqoli Khan, as well as Natavan and her sons; recent archaeological studies have confirmed that the area has been used as a burial ground since ancient times, tracing the earliest tombs back to the time when Azerbaijan was part of Caucasian Albania, between the fourth century BCE and the eighth century AD.

It was near the ancient family tomb of the khans of Karabakh that the Imaret Stadionu was built in 1951; the stadium's name can be translated as palace, but also as castle or fortress. Imaret became the home of Mehsul, the football club that was founded in the city of Agdam in the same year.

Apart from the presence of the family tomb of the khans of the Javanshir dynasty in Imaret, the ancient history of Agdam is lost in the mists of uncertainty and, in part, of legend. What is certain is that Agdam was home to a two-storey palace belonging to Khasay Khan Usmiyev, Natavan's husband; also, between 1751 and 1752, Panah Ali Khan built the Shahbulag Castle – literally, the king's spring residence – near Agdam, before moving the capital to Shusha. The fortress is still visible and can be visited. In the 13th century, the army of Jalaluddin, son of Muhammad II, last ruler of the Chorasmian Empire (or Khwarezm Shah), settled for a period in Agdam; on 28 July 1402, Timur won an important victory against the Ottoman Sultan Bayezid I at the Battle of Ancyra (now Ankara) and rested his army for two years in the Agdam region. An article by the historian Nariman Babayev in *Lenin Yolu* – a newspaper once published in Agdam – entitled 'Tarixi keçmişimizdən' ('From Our History') recalls that in the *Afzal al-Tawarikh* – a chronicle written in the Persian language in 1617 that tells the story of the Safavid dynasty from 1501 – the author Fazli Isfahani includes several important details about Arran, Barda, Agdam, Gabala and other locations in Karabakh, his native region. Isfahani recounts having visited Agdam more than once.

Sources that date the foundation of Agdam to 1741 or 1752 are therefore inaccurate; the city grew considerably during the time of the khan's khanate, in step with the local ruler's authority. During the period of Tsarist dominion, Agdam developed as an important centre for trade, as a city with a vocation for exchange, taking advantage of its position at a crossroads and proximity to Iran. Traders from all directions found no specific environmental obstacles blocking their route to Agdam, neither in summer nor winter. From this moment on, the story of the history of the city, as of all Nagorno-Karabakh, takes a delicate turn. Armenian and Azerbaijani sources clash, playing on differing translations of individual terms that grant birthright over the land to one or other of the peoples to justify reason in the conflict and self-justify their crimes. I will not stray into a narrative quagmire that would risk taking me into unexplored territories of rights and wrongs dripping with blood. I will instead limit myself to recounting the facts in the most objective way possible, going beyond the stories that tell of the Armenianisation of the Albanian people, of Tsarist decisions to populate traditional Azerbaijani areas with Armenian people, or of territories that belonged to the Armenian ruler Tigranes the Great in the first century BC.

The strategic position of a continuous coming and going of traders and caravans fostered the development and growth of handicrafts, the construction of public buildings and cultural exchange.

Agdam first received city status in 1828. This is how the location was described in the *TSB*, the *Great Soviet Encyclopaedia*:

'Agdam, the city, the centre of the district of Agdam in the SSR of Azerbaijan, at the eastern foot of the Karabakh range, on the edge of the Karabakh plain. Railway station, site of main roads. 18,000 inhabitants (1968). Production of oil, winemaking, canning, storage warehouses and tool factories. Technical schools: agriculture and agricultural mechanisation, medical and musical schools. Theatre. Founded in the mid-18th century, it was established as a city in 1828.'

A clarification that will turn out to be useful in the coming pages: Agdam was not and is not part of what is traditionally recognised as the territory of Nagorno-Karabakh, but has always been regarded as the gateway to Karabakh.

In 2011, the writer Vahid Qazi published a book entitled *Ruhlar şəhəri* [City of Ghosts], a collection of stories that describe something that no longer exists today, the life and people of Agdam, whose stones, as Ramiz Rovshen writes, are not made of stone.

Chapter 6 of Qazi's book is a story that focuses on the Imaret Stadium in the memories of the writer's youth, giving you the opportunity to breathe in the football of those years, but also providing a glimpse of the features of a city that no longer exists.

The writer talks about how the local team, Shafag, played their football league games at the stadium but also how it was central to other events, 'Celebrations in Agdam would be held at the Bread Museum or the House of Culture, but would alwaysend at the Imaret Stadium.'

The journey from home to the stadium is described in vivid detail, naming the various landmarks on the way, 'To get to the stadium from our neighbourhood, we had to cross the street known as 28 aprel küçəsi (28 April Street), which splits Agdam in half, from the Baku-Gazak motorway, which starts in a square in the city of Yevlax, along Barda's main thoroughfare to Stepanakert. We also had to pass Kamil's bakery (the war hadn't started then and his son hadn't been martyred yet), across the square in front of Agdam's theatre, the Lenin Gardens and towards the meat processing factory, through the unique and famous Çay Evin (Tea House), which had once been the only functioning mosque in the region during the Soviet Union.'

The spectators at the Imaret were a fundamental part of every match, the writer describing one such occasion when 'The stadium was at boiling point. Kids would come together in small groups and five or ten of them were getting ready to target a particular player ... As soon as the referee blew the whistle for the start of the second half, the stadium became a free for all. Screams from the stands and shouting from kids on the touchlines prevented the opposition from playing and they lost a lot of easy balls. Their goalkeeper didn't know whether to watch the game, the ball or the kids behind the goal.'

5

From Mehsul to Qarabag

THE EARLY years of football in Agdam were decidedly tough. After the club was founded in 1951, the biggest obstacles came with building a team capable of competing in the professional leagues of the Soviet Union championship, the structure of which changed several times in the course of its history.

The pyramid of its various levels was topped by the Vysshaya Liga, the first division, in which between 16 and 18 teams from all over the USSR took part. Immediately below it was the Pervaja Liga 2, with 22 teams, and together these two divisions represented the professional levels. The third step on the ladder consisted of the Vtoraya Liga, divided into zones: the third and fourth levels of the pyramid consisted, in practice, of the national championships of the individual SSRs.

An Azerbaijani team, from the city of Baku, took part in the Soviet championship for the first time in 1932. In 1938, Temp Baku was the first Azerbaijani team to compete in the Vysshaya Liga, finishing in

19th place out of 26 teams and being relegated as a consequence.

Three Azerbaijani teams played in the top flight of the Soviet Union league – in addition to Temp Baku, Dinamo Kirovabad in 1968 and, first and foremost, Neftchi Baku, with 27 participations and a third-place finish in 1966, the best-ever result for a team from the Azerbaijan SSR.

In the distant past of football in Agdam, we know only that a team from the city was chosen to represent Azerbaijan in a tournament in Sadovsky – in the Oblast of Odessa – and that the team from Agdam later succeeded in finishing second in a tournament held in Tatarbunary, in which 38 teams took part.

Prior to 1987, the team from the city of Agdam had changed its name three times. It played as Mehsul from 1951 to 1977, as Shafag from 1977 to 1982, and as Kooperator from 1982. In 1966, Mehsul finished fourth in their first-ever involvement in the Azerbaijan national championship, achieving their best result in 1968 by finishing second behind Merkezi Ordu Idman Klubu Baku, the Azerbaijan army team, who had been champions in 1962.

After playing for four consecutive years, however, the club withdrew from competition in the late 1960s due to a lack of financial support. They had had a similar problem in the early days, when it had taken 15 years to achieve sufficient financial stability to register for the championship. Despite this, the team representing the city continued to compete, even during the dark years, which lasted for almost a decade. One name in particular stood out during that period, a name that will soon return in this story in disruptive fashion.

Allahverdi Bagirov captained the team from Agdam against one from Jabrayil in the game for the Qızıl Sünbül (Golden Spike) Cup played in Fizuli. In 1976, Bagirov became the manager of the team, which was refounded the following year with the name Shafag and returned to compete in the Azerbaijan league. Leadership of the club was in the hands of Akbar Rustamov and the best result of that period was a fourth-place finish in the USSR championship. In 1982, as already mentioned, the club changed its name to Kooperator Agdam.

The real turning point in the city's footballing destiny came in 1987 when, in response to the unrest that was bubbling up in Nagorno-Karabakh, the club took the name we know today: FK Qarabag Agdam. Kooperator were on the pitch at the Imaret against Inshaatchi Sabirabad; the game ended in a 2-1 defeat for the home team. It was then that the local party secretary, Sadig Murtuzaev, decided the time had come to build a strong team to represent the whole Karabakh region. Elbur Abbasov, then director of Kooperator, suggested the name Qarabag. Obtaining approval for the club's new name, which represented its vocation as a team for the whole oblast, was not easy. Abbasov had to go right to the top of the party in Baku for final authorisation. It was pointed out to him that there was already a club named Karabakh in Khankendi (Stepanakert), but the former player insisted that the team from Agdam could only be called Qarabag and, after a protracted debate, consent for the new name was finally received.

When Bagirov was born in Agdam on 22 April 1946, his parents, after giving birth to seven daughters, decided to name their son Allahverdi, meaning 'a gift from God', a name he shared with his maternal grandfather. There are plenty of stories about Allahverdi Bagirov's childhood that, at times, have similar traits to those of apocryphal, hagiographic writings; what is certain is that during his adolescence and youth the young man from Agdam shone in the sporting arena, especially when it came to volleyball and athletics, and his talents allowed the various teams representing the city to succeed in regional competitions. Football, however, was his true sporting vocation: after distinguishing himself with the city's team in various tournaments, he agreed to take on the role of manager at what would become FK Qarabag Agdam.

Charismatic and authoritative, he only had to take to the pitch to silence the noisy Imaret crowd and calm spirits during and after defeats.

Vahid Qazi wrote in *Ruhlar şəhəri* that: 'If the manager had been someone other than Allahverdi Bagirov, it would have been impossible to stop the fans during difficult matches at the stadium. Once, players from one of his teams, known as Damjili at the time, lost in Gazakh and the bus windows were destroyed. The whole city was desperately waiting for the rematch for a chance at revenge. However, one word from Allahverdi and not even a single player was hit.'

Little has been written about Allahverdi Bagirov's time as a player or manager at Qarabag, but there are plenty of people who can talk about their own personal experiences of someone who would go on to become one of Azerbaijan's national heroes. Qazi told me about him in an interview, 'Allahverdi Bagirov is one of the symbols of the city of Agdam. He was captain of the team and its manager. He also went on to sponsor the club. The money he earned from the restaurants and other businesses he owned he spent on the team and, later, on his soldiers.'

'Before the war,' explained Vusal Agamirov, born and raised in Agdam, 'Bagirov had a restaurant in the city. I grew up eating the bread he baked on the restaurant's first floor. When we were kids, we would call it "Allahverdi çörəyi"; Allahverdi's bread.'

Agdam and bread, a special relationship between the city and the ancient and modern foodstuff that symbolically unites every culture and era of human history. Bread is the land; it is sweat and toil. Bread is work. The Çörək muzeyi, or Bread Museum, was opened in Agdam on 25 November 1983: its history, production techniques and processing tools formed the core of the displays in a museum housed in a former mill. Nothing happens by chance.

The idea behind the museum came from Sadig Murtuzaev, first secretary of the party district committee, who, in the space of just a year, restored the old mill, which dated back to the 19th century and had been built by Mohammad Garayev, a notable figure in the city's history. The museum complex also included a caravanserai.

The mill's façade was decorated with a series of colourful mosaics, designed by Zakir Rustamov, an artist from Agdam, and made by a team led by Eduard

Krupkin, appointed by the Department of Arts of the Ministry of Culture and by Sariya Ismayilova, head of the Museum Department.

The display was the second largest in the world, the largest in the entire USSR. It was protected by the Azerbaijan SSR as cultural heritage and included 2,800 items from all over the Soviet Union, including grains of wheat dating from the seventh century BC. The mill continued to operate until 1987, allowing visitors to experience the local product first-hand.

The Armenian armed forces attacked the museum twice, but the first rocket failed to explode. The second missile hit its target on 12 August 1992 at 4.40pm, as reported by the Karabakh Interdistrict Prosecutor's Office's chief investigator Zahid Valiyev. Nothing could be done: fire broke out and spread throughout the building, destroying some 1,500 artefacts and bringing the story of Agdam's Bread Museum to an end.

Yukha, yayma, fatir, lavash, sangak, khamrali, fasali, kata, tandir, khorakli, bayim and *lezgin* are just some of the many names for bread in Azerbaijan, the names it also used to have in Agdam. Varieties, different leavening and baking techniques: a mosaic of flavours and aromas that spread throughout the city's streets, before the war broke out.

Unusually, Karabakh cuisine offers many variations on specific dishes; the same dish is, in fact, prepared and cooked in different ways in the various regions. Soups, for example: in the variant found in the Agdam region, potatoes, rice or pasta, cherry plums, plums and dried dogwood are added to the meat, while in the Jabrayil region, beans are used, and in Aghjabadi people prefer to use chicken broth instead. We have come across a similarity in traditional Azerbaijani variants of hadik polenta grains: in the Khojavend region, for example, peas or beans are added to the dish, as are boiled millet and onions fried in oil. The population of the Lachin region, on the other hand, adds only dogwood and dried apples to the dish.

The Agdam variation of meat soup is as follows:

300g beef on the bone
1 onion
60ml oil
200g potatoes
50g rice or pasta
50g dried cherry plums
50g dried plums
50g dried dogwood
30g tomato paste
Salt and pepper to taste

Boil the meat before adding to a pan and frying in oil with the onions. Add the tomato paste, meat broth, rice, pasta, potatoes and dried fruits and cook together. Shortly before serving, add salt, pepper and aromatic herbs to taste. Chicken soup is prepared in the same way.

6

Black January and independence

Baku, 23 November 2018
Elmler Akademiyasi

A stop on metro line 2, in front of the Azerbaijan Academy of Sciences. Rustam and I meet in the early afternoon, the day after Qarabag's 4-0 defeat at Baku's Olympic Stadium, the address of which is 323, Heydar Aliyev Avenue. The stadium even has its own street number, making doubly sure no one has any excuse for missing the modern, gleaming cathedral in the glass desert that rises up out of nowhere to the west of the capital.

It's not far from the intersection that leads to the airport, also named after former president Heydar Aliyev, father of current president Ilham Aliyev. I had landed there three nights earlier at 8pm on Turkish Airlines flight TK334 from Istanbul, after connecting from Milan Malpensa. As we approached the city, I could clearly make out from the plane window a bright red illuminated ring, with the word Hyundai rotating around it in large lettering. Maybe it was a dress rehearsal for the Champions League game, or perhaps simply a dutiful display for the generous South Korean sponsor who has provided Azerbaijani sport with financial backing since the costly expenditure of around €700m for the construction of the facility to host the first European Games in 2015. In what may well have been a coincidence, the initial project drawn up by the Turkish TOCA (The Office of Contemporary Architecture) in 2010 was modified during construction in late 2012 by Heerim, an architecture and design company from South Korea. Just like Hyundai.

Whatever the case, I hadn't travelled to Elmler Akademiyasi in a South Korean car, but on bus number 18 from the stop at Icherisheher, near my hotel, just outside the walls of the Old City. The name of that metro station is, in fact, composed of two words: Icheri Sheher, meaning Old Town. In 2000, UNESCO listed the 'Walled City of Baku with the Shirvanashan's Palace and Maiden Tower' as a World Heritage Site.

We stop for a takeaway dessert in a small pastry shop Rustam knows well, in an area teeming with students. We then take the same bus number 18 that brought me to Elmler, this time in the direction of the Flame Towers. The three skyscrapers of different heights, visible from all over the city, have become one of the most recognisable symbols of the new Azerbaijan. Flame Tower 1 is 33 floors and 190 metres high; Flame Tower 2 is 30 floors and 160 metres high; while the lowest, Flame Tower 3, is 28 floors and 140 metres high.

The façades of the towers – opened in April 2012 and intended for residential use – are one of the most popular sights with tourists and the city's population as a whole.

More than 10,000 high-powered LED lights supplied by Osram transform them into giant screens that project scrolling images every night, such as the national flag or advertisements for important events taking place in the city.

But we're not going to the towers, even if that's where bus number 18 leaves us.

'You can't write a book about Qarabag Agdam without visiting Shehidler Khiyabani,' Arthur told me that night we went out to play pool with Rustam and his friend Azhdars. A former journalist who had turned his back on his profession, Azhdars had chosen to move to Kazakhstan, his wife's homeland, to work for an oil company instead of signing a letter that would essentially end his freedom of expression at the newspaper he worked for. Censorship, simply.

I took Rustam at his word and followed blindly. I wasn't all that sure where we were going, what that strange name meant or why my two colleagues – one Dutch, the other Azerbaijani – had insisted I go there. Arthur didn't come with us because he had already seen the place on several occasions.

During the Soviet era, the park had been known as Kirov Park; since 21 January 1990 it had become Shehidler Khiyabani, Martyrs' Lane.

'I'm going to tell you a story,' says Rustam, adopting a serious tone and looking me square in the face as we walk along the avenue, among the gravestones carved with depictions of the dead and trees lined up in orderly rows like a funeral procession.

'I'm listening,' I reply.

'Do you know who Heydar Aliyev was?'

'Yes. The former president of Azerbaijan,' I answer.

'Not only that,' adds Rustam. 'Heydar Aliyev was a member of the Politburo in Moscow, one of the most important, to the extent that he became first deputy chairman of the Soviet Union under President Yuri Andropov.

'In the USSR and the mechanisms with which the machine worked, it was traditional for the designated heir to officiate at the president's funeral and for the secession to belong to them. Aliyev was the number one candidate to become president, but surprisingly, Gorbachev was appointed instead.

'I didn't know Aliyev was one step away from becoming head of the Soviet Union!' I say, not hiding my amazement but asking myself how much of what Rustam was telling me was historical truth and how much was the result of Azerbaijani propaganda.

'I tell him to go on, because the story is still interesting and, above all, I want him to tell me what this place he had brought me to and where we were walking represented.

Rustam continues, 'It wouldn't have been possible. They would never have allowed it in Moscow, even if it was rightfully his!'

'Why?'

'Can you imagine the first Muslim president of the Soviet Union back in 1985? Gorbachev was much better. He managed to force Aliyev to resign from the Politburo in 1985, along with other Brezhnev loyalists. At the time it was put down to ill health.'

A few more steps and Rustam tells me whose tombstones are on the avenue, 'It was like what happened in Prague during the famous spring. In January 1990, Gorbachev himself sent the Red Army here to Baku to put an end to a series of peaceful protests by the people of Azerbaijan, who wanted independence from Moscow, even after the slap in the face dished out to our leader Heydar Aliyev.'

'What happened?'

'The commander of the troops that entered the city gave an ultimatum: if they didn't take down the barricades and return to their homes by midnight, he would be forced to open fire on the demonstrators. According to estimates, between 133 and 137 people died; these are the tombstones that remember them, all of them.

'The martyrs of Azerbaijan, unarmed civilians killed by bullets fired by an army that was supposed to protect them.'

'Did the order to shoot come from Moscow?' I ask Rustam, trying to understand the true nature of Gorbachev, commonly considered a man of peace.

'There's no doubt that a Red Army commander wouldn't have been able to open fire on civilians without authorisation from the supreme leadership of the USSR,' Rustam continues. 'That's why I've never been able to understand how they managed to give Gorbachev the Nobel Peace Prize. To us he's a criminal, a murderer.'

Fariza is dressed in white, as a bride. She's not alone on the tombstone, but next to her husband Ilham, the couple immortalised on their wedding day. Fariza was 19 when Soviet tanks entered Baku and killed her 27-year-old husband on 20 January 1990. On the day of Ilham's funeral, Fariza took advantage of everyone's distraction – after having tried to set herself on fire a few days earlier – and killed herself. 'Don't cry. I couldn't be without Ilham. Mum, don't cry', were the words she wrote before ending her life to be reunited with her sweetheart. The date on which Ilham and Fariza got married, 30 June, has become Azerbaijan's own Valentine's Day.

Rustam and I proceed in silence towards the Eternal Flame Memorial, overlooking the vast panorama of the Caspian Sea.

* * *

Joint resolution of the Armenian SSR and Nagorno-Karabakh Oblast on reunification 1 December 1989

Proceeding from the universal principles of national self-determination and acceding to legal aspiration for reunification of the two segments of the Armenian people torn apart by force, the Armenian Supreme Soviet recognises the fact of NKAO's self-determination, and the congress of the plenipotentiary representatives of the NKAO and the National Council it has elected as the sole legal authority in force in the oblast. The Armenian Supreme Soviet and NKAO National Council declare the reunification of the Armenian Republic and the NKAO. The Armenian republic citizenship rights extend over the population of the NKAO. The Supreme Soviet and the National Council hereby set up a joint commission to formulate practical steps to realise reunification. They assume the obligation to represent the national interests of the Armenian population in northern Artsakh (NKAO), Shaumian rayon and Getashen districts.

The response from Azerbaijan was not slow in coming, arriving five days after the joint resolution of the Armenian SSR and the Nagorno-Karabakh Oblast. The judgement of the Azerbaijan Supreme Soviet was tough and clear. It expressed itself as follows:

Decision of the Supreme Soviet of the Azerbaijan SSR in connection with the decision of the Supreme Soviet of the Armenian SSR on uniting the Armenian SSR and the NKAO.

Baku, 6 December 1989
The decision adopted by the Armenian SSR Supreme Soviet on 1 December 1989 to unite the Armenian SSR and NKAO is regarded as an impermissible interference in the Sovereign Azerbaijan SSR's affairs and a measure aimed at encroaching on the Azerbaijan SSR's territorial integrity, which does not contribute toward the effort made to stabilise the situation in the region and restore normal conditions.

Unfortunately, the reaction from Azerbaijan was not limited to words, but extended to the unleashing of a wave of violence and pogroms against the Armenian population throughout the territory of the SSR. Armenians were violently expelled from the city of Baku, which found itself poised to become the scene of the final confrontation between Moscow and the Popular Front, the movement founded by Abulfaz Elchibey to carry on the struggle for Azerbaijan's independence from Soviet rule. It is estimated that before the events of 1988, the request for incorporation into the Armenian SSR by the NKAO and the Sumgait pogroms, there were about 200,000 Armenians in Baku; on the eve of 1990, with the latest episodes of violence perpetrated against them by Azerbaijanis angered by the territorial manoeuvres at the expense of the Azerbaijan SSR, this figure had been reduced to between 30,000 and 40,000.

In December, a group of Azerbaijanis living along the Iran border cut the fences at the frontier, demanding the establishment of closer relations with Iranian Azeris, in the name of shared origins. The administrations of Jalilabad and Lankaran surrendered to the rebellions, handing over the local government to the Popular Front of Azerbaijan.

* * *

Independence from Moscow and the defence of Azerbaijan's sovereignty from Armenian demands was the uncompromising platform declared by Elchibey's PFA (Popular Front of Azerbaijan), although it failed to specify ways or means to pursue its objective.

On 9 January 1990, the Armenian parliament voted to include Nagorno-Karabakh within its budget; fighting broke out between Armenians and Azerbaijanis in the villages of the Khanlar and Shaumian regions, in northern Azerbaijan.

In addition to the growing hatred that was exploding between the two populations, another element was now inevitably on the table of a conflict that had yet to find its greatest outlet.

Moscow no longer controlled Nagorno-Karabakh and Azerbaijan, which was one step away from leaving the union. Worried by the Baku pogroms and the demonstrations that contained a loud cry for independence, Gorbachev attempted a diplomatic move to regain control of the situation on the Caspian Sea: the sending of a delegation directly from the Politburo, headed by his close political ally Yevgeny Primakov. Soviet Defence Minister Dmitry Yazov also went to Baku to take command of the tens of thousands of soldiers encamped just outside the city.

The streets of Baku were in the hands of PFA activists, who erected barricades with cars, buses, lorries and concrete blocks along the roads that accessed the barracks located on the edge of the city; the Soviet central authorities evacuated the men sent by them to manage the situation, and local officials, moving them to military command posts in the suburbs.

Primakov told the PFA leaders he would not tolerate Azerbaijan's secession from the Soviet Union and implicitly threatened the use of force, although, as Etibar Mamedov reported to Thomas De Waal, in a phone call with Gorbachev, he tried to convince him not to authorise military intervention.

On 19 January, a state of emergency was introduced in Baku and other regions of the Azerbaijan SSR by a decree signed by Gorbachev. This was the leverage that allowed for what, by that stage, appeared horrifyingly inevitable. The soldiers entered the city on the night between 19 and 20 January, acting on the basis of the state of emergency proclaimed by the president of the USSR, who authorised the intervention after consultation with his lieutenants on the outskirts of the city. Soviet special forces took out the local television station, blowing it up at 7.30pm, as well as the telephone lines, making communications and the widespread dissemination of the news of the state of emergency impossible. As a result, many only became aware of the measure the following morning, by which time the streets were full of corpses. Shortly after midnight, 26,000 Soviet soldiers forced their way into Baku, crushed the barricades with tanks, destroying cars and even ambulances. They fired on civilians, their civilians, killing between 133 and 137, according to estimates. The victims also included at least 21 Soviet soldiers, leading Gorbachev to say that his soldiers had opened fire against armed opposition; in reality, it seems to have been established that the PFA resistance was unarmed and that the soldiers may have been victims of friendly fire, the flurry of bullets flying in every direction on a night as red as blood and as black as lead. Qara Yanvar, Black January.

It was the first time the Soviet army had taken one of its own cities by force, a tragedy for Azerbaijan and for the Soviet Union as a whole, if it still made sense to consider it as such. It only took the soldiers a few hours to regain control of the city and restore the order established by the Moscow authorities. But on 20 January 1990, Moscow effectively lost Azerbaijan. The entire population of Baku took to the streets for the mass funeral of the victims of Black January, who immediately became, in the collective perception, the first martyrs of the new Azerbaijan; thousands of members of the Communist Party publicly burned their membership cards.

The party officials who resigned in open protest at the barbaric violence perpetrated against those demonstrating for independence included Heydar Aliyev. He went on to ride the wave of discontent of the Azerbaijani people to return to the political stage, after more than two years of forced exile in his native Nakhchivan.

On 7 February 1990, the Central Committee of the CPSU accepted Gorbachev's recommendation that the party renounce its monopoly on political power. In the same year, the first competitive elections were held in all the then republics of the USSR and the opposition to the Communist Party succeeded in taking its place in the national soviets for the first time, while the various reformist and ethnic nationalist parties won a large number of seats. The CPSU lost the elections in six Soviet Socialist Republics: on 24 February, after a four-day ballot, the Sąjūdis won in Lithuania, while the following day, the Popular Front of Moldova won the election in Moldova. The Popular Fronts of Estonia and Latvia achieved a majority in their respective republics in the electoral round of 18 March.

Elections were held in Armenia on 20 May, with further rounds on 3 June and 15 July. These were won by the Pan-Armenian National Movement (HHSh), an offshoot of the Karabakh Committee, a champion of requests for annexation. Finally, the Round Table-Free Georgia coalition won a majority in the Georgian Soviet following the 28 October election, which ended with the 11 November run-off.

The giant with feet of clay was now staggering with nothing to grab on to; its fall was inevitable and imminent.

A powerful shove was provided by the three Baltic republics of Estonia, Latvia and Lithuania, which – following the election results that clearly rewarded three independence groups that pushed the old granite communist apparatus into a minority – proclaimed their independence from the Soviet Union.

The death of the Soviet bear was hastened by the coup d'état in August 1991. Having taken note of the electoral result in the 15 SSRs, Gorbachev had planned a series of reforms that would have concretely responded to requests for greater autonomy and dealt with the rapidly changing times more generally.

Art. 72: Each republic shall retain the right freely to secede from the USSR.
(Constitution of the Union of Soviet Socialist Republics, Moscow, Kremlin, 7 October 1977).

No republic had ever implemented Article 72 of the constitution before Estonia, Latvia and Lithuania's unilateral declarations of independence. In Moscow's corridors of power, it may never even have been considered that someone might one day want to use this passe-partout, provided for by the fundamental law of the union, running the risk of creating a chain of secessions that would have sanctioned the end of the USSR. Or perhaps it had, given that historians often spoke of secret plans for a controlled end to the Soviet Union, for an emancipation of the republics considered plausible in the wake of the event that upset all the cards on the table in the politics of the Communist bloc countries: the collapse of the Berlin Wall on 9 November 1989.

Gorbachev supported the USSR law of 3 April 1990, known as the Law on Secession, in an attempt to put a stop to the expected departure of the republics; in it he instituted a new procedure for leaving the union, establishing the need to hold popular referendums in particular. On 28 June 1991, he declared the COMECON dissolved, before doing the same with the Warsaw Pact on 1 July; but the real move that would have changed the substance of the USSR forever was the New Treaty of the Union, which the president was supposed to sign on 20 August 1991. This document would sanction the transformation of the Soviet Union into a federation of independent republics with a common president.

To prevent the ratification of the treaty, eight of Moscow's highest-ranking officials, including Gorbachev's deputy Gennady Yanayev, Prime Minister Valentin Pavlov, Defence Minister Dmitry Yazov, Interior Minister Boris Pugo, and the head of the KGB Vladimir Kryuchkov, formed the State Committee on the State of Emergency and, on 19 August, detained President Gorbachev against his will at his dacha in the Crimea.

What would become known as the August Putsch, a coup d'état, was under way, but would fail miserably. Boris Yeltsin, president of the Russian Soviet Federative Socialist Republic (SFSR), led the resistance from Moscow's White House – seat of the Russian parliament – with the support of the people, who took to the streets against the coup leaders. Standing on a tank in the middle of a crowded Red Square with a megaphone, Yeltsin condemned the coup leaders. In the night between 21 and 22 August, Gorbachev was sent back to Moscow by plane and the armoured vehicles withdrew, declaring the failure of the attempted coup. Seven of the members of the so-called Gang of Eight were arrested, while Pugo committed suicide before he could be captured.

Gorbachev took back the presidential reins, but, instead of strengthening the Soviet Union, the failed coup only hastened its end. By now, the leader was alone in command; top-ranking officials and structures no longer listened to him. The 'Wind of Change', as West German rock band Scorpions sang back then, could not be stopped and continued to blow ever stronger.

On 27 August, the European Union recognised the independence of Estonia, Latvia and Lithuania; in Kyiv, the Ukrainian parliament voted for independence and called a popular referendum, in paradoxical conformity with the Law on Secession of 3 April 1990, for 1 December. On 24 August 1991, Mikhail Gorbachev resigned as general secretary of the Communist Party of the Soviet Union; he formally remained as president of the USSR until Christmas evening, when he announced his resignation on live television. These are the final sentences spoken by Gorbachev as president of the USSR: 'Of course, there were mistakes made that could have been avoided, and many of the things that we did could have been done better. But I am positive that sooner or later, our common efforts will bear fruit and our nations will live in a prosperous, democratic society. I wish everyone all the best.'

Then, that same evening, the red flag with the hammer and sickle was lowered from the highest flagpole in the Kremlin and replaced with the red, white and blue flag of the Russian Federation. A Tsarist heirloom.

It was the end of the Soviet Union, the dissolution of which was ratified by the Supreme Soviet, which met for the last time on 26 December 1991.

7

From the end of the USSR to the fall of Agdam

AZERBAIJAN FOLLOWED the wave of secessions that came in the wake of the August coup and declared itself independent from the Soviet Union on 30 August 1991.

A constitutional act proclaiming independence read:

'The Supreme Council of the Republic of Azerbaijan on the basis of the Declaration of Independence of the National Council of Azerbaijan of 28 May 1918, the democratic principles of the Republic of Azerbaijan and the inheritance of traditions and adhering to the declaration of the Supreme Council of the Republic of Azerbaijan of 30 August, 1991. On the restoration of the state independence of the Republic of Azerbaijan approved the present Constitutional Act and established the state system, the political and economic

structure of the independent Republic of
Azerbaijan.'

Three days later, on 2 September, the Council of the
Nagorno-Karabakh Autonomous Oblast, in joint
session with the Shahoumian regional council, declared
its secession from the independent Azerbaijan and
proclaimed the birth of the 'Nagorno Karabakh Republic
within the borders of the current Nagorno-Karabakh
Autonomous Oblast and neighbouring Shahoumian
region (Abr. NKR)'.

The third stakeholder waited a few more days before
entering the fray, but, inevitably, on 23 September,
Armenia also declared itself independent: the macabre
dance, the death ritual, could begin.

The first real act of war occurred on 20 November,
when an Azerbaijani Soviet-made Mil Mi-8 military
helicopter was shot down near the village of Karakend,
in Nagorno-Karabakh's Khojavend province. The
aircraft had taken off from Agdam and was carrying a
delegation charged with monitoring the situation in the
area, as part of the agreement signed in Zheleznovodsk
on 23 September between the leaders of Russia and
Kazakhstan for a peaceful resolution of the Nagorno-
Karabakh conflict. Armenian militias fired on the Mi-8
with ZSU-23-4 Shilka and SA-6 missiles, killing all 22
people on board. In addition to the three crew members,
13 Azerbaijani government officials lost their lives in
Karakend, including the secretary of state, the public
prosecutor general, the deputy prime minister, two
Russian observers, the Kazakhstani deputy minister of

internal affairs as well as three Azerbaijani journalists. It was a massacre that extinguished any budding hope of dialogue and peace.

The political response was not long in coming and, on 26 November, the Parliament of Azerbaijan declared the autonomy of Nagorno-Karabakh abolished and, as a tangible sign of greater and more effective control over the region, restored the ancient name of Khankendi in place of Stepanakert. On 10 December, the Armenians of Nagorno-Karabakh voted in a referendum to ratify the birth of the NKR.

'Do you agree that the proclaimed Nagorno-Karabakh Republic should be an independent state acting on its own authority to decide forms of cooperation with other states and communities?' The referendum question was provided in three languages: Armenian, Azerbaijani and Russian. The result was a resounding endorsement: the 'yes' vote received 108,615 votes, equal to 99.98 per cent, with 'no' chosen by only 24 voters, equal to just 0.02 per cent.

Everything was falling ruinously into an abyss of violence and destruction. And it was doing so with a political overture, with the feeling that, as had been the case in other republics, the issue could still be resolved through elections or the courts, in a non-violent way somehow. But this was not true; everyone was clear on what was about to happen. Because it was already happening.

By late 1991, Nagorno-Karabakh was slowly building its own army. Only a dozen military units had been established in the self-proclaimed independent republic, most of them armed only with shotguns or improvised weapons.

At that time, Shusha was still an Azeri city. Azerbaijan's regular army used the fortified city, the ancient capital of the Karabakh Khanate, as a preferred location from which to launch missiles and bullets on Stepanakert, capital of the self-proclaimed NKR. Or on Khankendi. Same difference. Or perhaps not, given what I have already said about the weight of words and their crucial importance in this conflict. Speaking of which, for the Armenians and Karabatsi, Shusha is known as Shushi.

Since December, batteries of BM-21 missiles – known by a sadly too oft repeated and notorious name in this conflict, Grad – had been used to bomb Stepanakert, along with modified Alazan weather-control rockets.

On 26 January 1992, the Azerbaijani army attacked the village of Karintak, south of Shusha, and the Karabatsi resistance forced them to leave dozens of victims on the battlefield, at least 60 according to reports from TASS, the Russian news agency.

* * *

Corriere della Sera, Tuesday 3 March 1992
Karabakh, the hills of horror
Discovery of dozens of mutilated and
skinned corpses
MOSCOW – At least 50 corpses of inhabitants of Khojaly – the Azeri town taken on Wednesday by the Armenians – have been discovered on the hills surrounding the Armenian city of Askeran.

Most were old men, women and children, often
with crushed skulls, a sign of shots fired at close
range. Some of the bodies had been mutilated,
others even skinned.

One of the most heinous massacres of this bloody war took
place on 25 and 26 February. In Khojaly, on the road from
Stepanakert to Agdam, at least 161 Azerbaijani civilians
were killed – according to the humanitarian organisation
Human Rights Watch – massacred by Armenian militias.
The description of the facts is confusing; each of the
parties involved has tried to shape the narrative of events
to their own advantage, or in their own defence, and
even international observers disagree when it comes to
telling an unequivocal version of what happened. The
incontrovertible fact is that the Azeri population of
Khojaly began fleeing the village besieged by Azerbaijani
militias. Human Rights Watch describes what happened
next, 'A large column of residents, accompanied by a
few dozen retreating fighters, fled the city as it fell to
Armenian forces. As they approached the border with
Azerbaijan, they came across an Armenian military post
and were cruelly fired upon.

'In the late summer and early autumn 1991 Armenians
fought to re-seize their villages, and Azerbaijanis used
force to counter Nagorno-Karabakh's declaration of
independence. The number of casualties and hostages
began to mount rapidly.

'After the formal break-up of the Soviet Union in
December 1991, USSR MVD troops, believed by some
to have had some mitigating effect on the hostilities,

withdrew from Nagorno-Karabakh, leaving Armenian and Azerbaijani forces in more open conflict with each other.

'The dissolution of the USSR also adversely affected control over, and discipline within, its armed forces. Heavy artillery, rocket-propelled grenades (RPGs), rocket launchers, tanks, armed personnel carriers, and the like, property of the Soviet Army, were either sold to, loaned to or otherwise found their way into the hands of combatants on both sides, making the armed conflict even more lethal.

'Karabakh erupted into full-scale war in 1992 as weapons poured into the region and Soviet Interior Ministry troops withdrew. The use of mercenaries on both sides was common, and many alleged that rogue Russian army units took part in combat.'

Armenians and Azerbaijanis both accused the Russians of helping their respective enemies and told stories of Russian commanders, at various levels, who would lease their troops and tanks to whichever of the two adversaries could pay them. Entering the realm of legend, common when it comes to military stories, some even spoke of individual tanks taking part in military actions for one of the two factions and then, the next day, for the other. Renting a T-72 combat tank with a crew of three was said to cost between US$100 and US$200. Ammunition was charged separately.

The Human Rights Watch explanation continued, 'Four major events characterised the war in 1992: the massacre of hundreds of Azeri civilians in Khojaly, NKAO, by Karabakh forces with alleged support of the

366th Regiment of the Russian army; the Karabakh Armenian seizure of Shusha, the last Azeri-populated town in Karabakh (it served as a fire base for attacks on Stepanakert); the Karabakh Armenian capture of the Azerbaijani town of Lachin and the six-mile "corridor" between Nagorno-Karabakh and Armenia; and the June 1992 Azerbaijani offensive against Mardakert province in Nagorno-Karabakh. Serious human rights violations by both sides characterised all the above actions.

'Both sides shelled each other's cities and towns and committed atrocities.

'In February 1992, Karabakh Armenian forces – reportedly backed by soldiers from the 366th Motor Rifle Regiment of the Russian Army – seized the Azeri-populated town of Khojaly, about seven kilometres outside of Stepanakert. More than 200 civilians were killed in the attack, the largest massacre to date in the conflict.

'In April, an Azerbaijani attack on Maraga reportedly took 40 civilian lives and several dozen hostages. A month later, the Karabakh Armenians – again with alleged Russian support – seized Shusha, Karabakh's last Azeri-populated town. Later that month, Karabakh Armenian forces broke through to Armenia at the Azerbaijani town of Lachin, creating the so-called Lachin corridor. At Lachin, roughly ten kilometres separates Armenia from Karabakh.

'In June 1992, however, a large-scale Azerbaijani offensive against the Geranboi (Shahoumian) region of Azerbaijan and Mardakert province in Nagorno-Karabakh achieved initial success. Armed with heavy weapons received after the division of the Soviet army's arsenal under the Treaty of Tashkent of May 1992, the Azeri army captured nearly 80 percent of Mardakert province and created nearly 40,000 ethnic Armenian refugees. The Azeri forces subjected the Armenians in Karabakh – including civilians – to a withering air and artillery bombardment during the summer of 1992. By September, however, the Karabakh Armenian position had stabilised.'

While the Armenians of Nagorno-Karabakh needed 1992 to take the Lachin corridor – strategically located for advancing on their motherland Armenia and stabilising their positions in the conflict – conquering Shusha and thus alleviating bombing in Stepanakert, 1993 was the year during which the victory was constructed. The year of the fall of Agdam.

'No one has ever pretended that Agdam was part of the Armenian homeland,' writes Markar Melkonian, the brother of the Armenian-American commander Monte, according to Goltz's *Azerbaijan Diary*. 'The battle for Agdam would be a battle for a bargaining chip, not a battle to defend our homeland.'

In mid-1993, however, Agdam undoubtedly assumed even greater strategic importance after the fall of Shusha, by now the only outpost from which Azerbaijani artillery could bomb Stepanakert.

On 12 June, the Armenian army of Nagorno-Karabakh began laying siege to the city of Agdam, which was under attack from three sides and subjected to continuous bombing for three weeks, with the population forced to flee along the only remaining escape route. Initially, the NKR forces denied they were interested in conquering the city, citing the desire to destroy positions that were the source of direct fire on their capital as the motivation for their attack.

The following day, *La Repubblica* reported that Armenian forces have launched a violent offensive against the Agdam region, in the Azerbaijani territory in the east of Nagorno-Karabakh, with an extremely high toll of dead and wounded, while peace negotiations between the Armenian and Azerbaijani authorities sponsored by the Conference on Security and Cooperation in Europe (CSCE) appear to have stalled. Sources close to the Azerbaijani presidency report that fierce fighting has taken place in the Agdam region, including with the use of aviation. The Armenian authorities in Nagorno-Karabakh, who were expected to express their opinion on the peace plan put forward by the Commission on Security and Cooperation in Europe on Friday, requested an extension following the emergence of differences between the political and military leadership of the enclave struggling for independence from Azerbaijan.

'On the day Agdam was occupied,' Vahid Qazi tells me, 'I was finishing my last day of work at the presidential administration. It was my final day as an official. The Armenians had been attacking for a few weeks. The city had never been attacked like that before. When the fighting reached Agdam, I could only communicate with the city through the telephone operator inside the post office. Now I'm ashamed to remember that woman I never saw. I think I will carry her voice with me until my dying day, "The Armenians will enter the city. They will take Agdam. They've abandoned us." When she didn't answer my next call, I knew the city had been occupied. It was the most tragic day of my life.'

After a moment's silence, he continues, 'Sometimes I still call the number of our house in Agdam. I still think my mother will pick up and answer.'

Agdam fell on 23 July 1993, under a hail of bullets and Grad missiles fired by the Karabatsi artillery. The Armenians did not even grant the city the honour of remembrance: they decided to raze it to the ground, completely. Not only subdued and conquered, but erased forever from the face of the earth, destroyed and annihilated.

Agdam was no more.

8

The Azerbaijan title and
the last game at the Imaret

'AGDAM WAS a beautiful city, with fertile ground for farming, fresh air, clean water and, most importantly, kind and courageous people.'

These words were spoken by Elshad Khudadatov, born in Agdam in 1965, who built his entire career as a footballer for Qarabag. He is echoed by Shahid Hasanov, born in 1957 and originally from Shusha, linchpin of the Qarabag defence since 1987, 'Agdam was a very beautiful and rich city in Azerbaijan. Everyone wanted to play for the team from that city. Life was normal and calm; everyone went about their business. Being in Agdam was amazing.'

'It was the pride of Karabakh,' explains the team's long-standing captain Sattar Aliyev. 'The air was fresh and the people were friendly.'

With these three players on the pitch, Qarabag Agdam FK won their first Azerbaijan SSR title in 1988, ahead of Pambigchi Barda and Stroitel Sabirabad. Elbrus Mammadov was the manager.

'When we won the league, we turned professional,' remembers Hasanov, 'and we won the right to play in the ninth zone of the Soviet Second Division.'

'In 1990, we won the domestic league again and found ourselves in the Soviet Second Division for the second time,' remembers Aliyev. 'We would play against teams from Ukraine, Moldova, Belarus and Russia; we represented Azerbaijan well.'

Qarabag also came away with the Azerbaijan Cup that year.

In the team's early years, Qarabag were sponsored by the city's grain industry. 'We didn't have presidents or vice-presidents back then,' explains Hasanov. 'The team set-up was just players and coaches. The goal at that time was to win the league and qualify for the top level of the Soviet league. But the city authorities always supported us, until we turned professional.'

Sajavus Farzaliyev was appointed club president; he was the director of Agdam's wine factory, which became the team sponsor. At that time, the city was most famous for, among other products, two types of fortified wine similar to cheap port, called '777' and one known simply as 'Agdam'. The latter was very popular throughout the Soviet Union and affordably priced. Back then, enthusiasts of this type of wine were known in Russia as 'Agdamshik'. Production levels at the wine factory were so great that it was one of the biggest backers of the city's finances.

Three indigenous grape varieties bear the name of the city of Agdam, according to *Caucasus and Northern Black Sea Region Ampelography*, 'Agdam Gyzyl Uzunu (Golden Grape of Agdam) is mainly used to make fortified sweet

"Porto" style wines and dry wines for brandy-making. The variety gives also good table wines, characterised by a slightly feeble taste, 10.0-12.0 per cent alcohol and 5.3-6.0 g/L-1t total acidity. The wines are usually used to make brandy. This variety is also used locally for the production of a very concentrated boiled grape juice called Bekmez (Doshab) and for making jam. Due to its good sensorial characteristics, this grape is also used for fresh consumption.

'Agdam Gyulabasi (Flower aroma – Gyulabi from Agdam) is suitable for making high-quality yellow-gold table wines. The variety is also suitable for making dessert wines.

'Agdam Khazarisi (Agdam Caspian Sea) is widely used as a table grape variety and for the production of a speciality called "Irchal" (concentrated grape juice with berries inside). Hanging grapes can be stored until March-April. This variety is suitable for long-term storage and transport. Under good storage conditions, taste and quantity of the grapes improves over time. Among all the main table grape varieties of Azerbaijan, "Agdam Khazarisi" is the most suitable for storage.'

That a traditionally Muslim country should have been dedicated to the production of wine may seem strange, but the tradition was not actually all that long-standing; the technique had developed after the October Revolution, when the Bolshevik leaders supplanted local Islamic religious leaders. In the early 1980s, Karabakh boasted 18,000 hectares of vineyards with an annual grape production of 165,000 tonnes. On 16 May 1985, Mikhail Gorbachev launched a campaign to limit alcohol consumption, with the aim of tackling the scourge of alcoholism so widespread in the Soviet Union. Measures taken included an increase in the price of alcoholic beverages, a cap on the sale of products and the destruction of vineyards used for the production of wine, in the Caucasian republics in particular. In addition, the sale of sugar was also rationed to avoid its use in bootleg distillation. All products were sold through special coupons, with a focus on vodka, by far the most widely consumed spirit in the USSR. Every individual could buy no more than two half-litre bottles of vodka per month. The presidential campaign cost Karabakh the destruction of 5,000 hectares of vineyards; the remaining 13,000 were later burned or abandoned during the war.

* * *

And then there was him. More than a footballer or a coach, a symbol for Agdam, for the whole of Azerbaijan: Allahverdi Bagirov.

'Bagirov,' Vahid Qazi explains, 'represents for Qarabag Agdam what Franz Beckenbauer represents for Bayern Munich.'

'A great manager with plenty of experience and quality. A real captain when he pulled on the Agdam team shirt,' remembers Shahid Hasanov. 'He taught sport at schools too, as well as guiding Qarabag from the bench.'

'I was a kid. I was 12 when Allahverdi, who was my manager, gave me a pair of football boots as a present. It was hard to find a pair back then,' says Mushfiq Huseynov, 'but he really cared about me and told me he could see a great future for me as a footballer.'

This is backed up by Mushfiq's older brother Yashar: 'He was my manager and, years before that, we played together too. He was my captain, but at the same time we also had a great relationship. He was very special to me, as a footballer, but also as a leader, for everything he's done for Agdam.'

In 1988, Allahverdi and his brother Eldar decided to join the fight for their land, to prevent Karabakh from falling into the hands of the Armenians. The first to hoist the flag of an independent Azerbaijan in the city of Agdam was none other than Allahverdi Bagirov, who, in October 1991, was one of the three commanders to whom the battalions defending Agdam within the fledgeling Azerbaijan army were assigned.

He was assigned military unit number 845; unit 836 was assigned to Shirin Mirzayev and unit 863 to Yagub Rzayev. Bagirov's *nom de guerre* was 'Gogha Gartal', Old Eagle.

Allahverdi's wife, Valide Bagirova, remembers one of the episodes that best describe the man, the soldier and future national hero of Azerbaijan; Bagirov personally took care of negotiating with the Armenian militias for the exchange of victims and prisoners of war following the Khojaly massacre.

'Before Khojaly, Allahverdi knew that there would be a tragedy there,' Valide told the journalist Robert O'Connor. 'But our defence ministers wouldn't allow him to go in there. The Russians, who we relied upon, didn't want for us to go because they never wanted Azerbaijan to be independent. They wanted our lands occupied, so they said no.'

Valide continued, 'Once the massacre began, Allahverdi didn't wait for orders'.He took his men and went to Khojaly anyway. He did it all himself. He saved 1,300 people from the Armenians at Khojaly, and he brought back hundreds of dead bodies from the area back to the mosque at Agdam. They were frozen from the cold.'

He managed to save and bring 1,300 Azerbaijanis back into the arms of their loved ones, including prisoners and the bodies of those killed during the massacre. His story is always blurred between truth and hagiography, between a factual telling of events and legend, as is often the case with heroes.

During the exchange on the border with the enemy-controlled territories, Bagirov suddenly embraced an Armenian prisoner. Staring into the camera the military operators Seyidaga Movsumli and Chingiz Mustafayev were using to film the scene, Bagirov explained that the man had been his team-mate at Agdam for several years; the Armenian looked at him and said, 'I hope we never find ourselves on opposing sides again.'

On 12 June 1992, the car in which Bagirov was travelling ran over an anti-tank mine on its way back to Agdam after he had recaptured the fortress of Askeran with a platoon of 150 men in January, replacing the Armenian flag with that of independent Azerbaijan. He died together with his driver and was buried in the cemetery in Agdam, next to his brother Eldar, who had been killed seven months earlier on the way back from a meeting of the Supreme Soviet in Baku, shot dead under circumstances that were never clarified.

When the Armenian commander with whom he had negotiated the prisoner exchanges, Vitali Balasanyan, learned of Allahverdi's death, he contacted the Azerbaijani soldiers by radio to ask for confirmation of the news. 'How could you not save a man like that?'

After his death, on 24 February 1993, Bagirov was awarded the title of 'National Hero of Azerbaijan' and later, by a decree signed by President Elchibey, the honour of the Golden Star.

The formal announcement was as follows:

A.T. Bagirov named 'National Hero of Azerbaijan'

THE PRESIDENT OF THE REPUBLIC OF AZERBAIJAN

For personal courage and dedication shown in protecting the sovereignty and territorial integrity of the Republic of Azerbaijan, and personal integrity and courage in defence of the civilian population, Allahverdi Teymur oglu Bagirov, commander of the military unit named after E. Bagirov, is named 'National Hero of Azerbaijan' (after his death).

President of the Republic of Azerbaijan Abulfaz Elchibey.

Baku, 24 February 1993.
476.

* * *

In Agdam, they carried on playing football, despite the blasts from the Grad rockets thundering in the sky overhead during Qarabag matches and the news from the front of the death of their former captain and manager Allahverdi Bagirov.

'It was one of the saddest moments of my life,' remembers Mushfiq, 'when I heard that Allahverdi had died. We found out when we were playing an away game in Zaqatala against Dashqin.'

In 1992, following independence from the now former Soviet Union, the newly founded Association of Football Federations of Azerbaijan (AFFA) oversaw the first domestic football league championship played, from 3 May to 20 October that same year. The format included two groups of 13 teams; in addition to relegation play-offs at the bottom of the table, the top two teams in each group would play off in semi-finals, and a final to decide the winner, always over two legs. A win for Neftchi, whose reign over Azerbaijani football was long-standing, went without saying.

The history of football in Azerbaijan is said to have started in 1911. At that time, British interest in Baku's oil, about which I have already said plenty, sparked the development of football in the Caucasian country. The constant influx of people from Britain, the historical birthplace of football, made the young sport popular with the locals. It was no coincidence that Baku's first football team was called the 'British Club'. The first official championship in Baku was held in 1911. Teams were funded primarily and founded by the oil companies, and the British Club were winners of the first championship.

As the number of football teams gradually increased, the Soviet leagues were organised with teams representing every city from 1922 to 1937, when it was established that participation in the championship should shift from city teams to actual clubs. At the time, there were teams representing a handful of industries or corporations; although Baku was a city with a vocation for oil, for which it was gaining fame throughout Europe, the sector's workers were still to get their own team. As it was, employees of the black gold industry decided to found their own football team. It didn't take them long to give it a name, choosing a word that acts as a reminder of its origins as the oil industry workers' team. Russian was the main language in workplaces across the USSR at that time, so their team was initially known as Neftyannik, a term that in the dominant language meant 'oil workers'.

The letters and symbols used on the team's strip also reflected the close affinity with the world of the oil workers: the H on the club crest represented the first letter of Neftyannik, written in Cyrillic characters. Black was to be the main colour of the shirt for a team that would come to be known commonly as Neftchi; the decision was taken to add white, to represent the so-called white gold; cotton, for the production of which Azerbaijan was as famous as it was for black gold.

In 1992, Qarabag Agdam began playing in the top division of the newly formed independent Azerbaijan football league. On 3 May 1992, in their opening game, Qarabag suffered their first and only home defeat in 23 league matches, 2-1 to Inshaatchi Sabirabad. The home side's only goal was scored by Mehman Alishanov in the fourth minute, the first goal in the history of the independent Azerbaijan league.

On 17 September 1992, the Azerbaijan national side took to the pitch for the first time in a friendly against Georgia in Tbilisi. Making their debut, which ended in a 6-3 defeat for Azerbaijan, were two players from Qarabag Agdam FK: Elshad Ahmadov and Zaur Garayev.

'We were horrified every time we took to the pitch during those months,' remembers Khudadatov. 'The Armenians would often attack the Imaret Stadium with Grad missiles while we were playing. Thank God the rockets never hit the stadium! The club's directors eventually decided we would train in Migachevir, 105km from Agdam.'

But they had to carry on playing matches there, at the Imaret Stadium, in Agdam. Qarabag had to stay among its people, because Qarabag was increasingly Karabakh; it was its people and it couldn't leave them on their own during their greatest test.

'We played our last game in Agdam in May 1993. As I say it, I've got tears in my eyes,' recalls an emotional Elshad Khudadatov.

'We trained under the bombing,' remembers Mushfiq Huseynov. 'There are no words to describe what we saw. Missiles flying over our heads while we played football; one day, I remember that a Grad hit the pitch and our terrified opponents bolted for the dressing room. We stayed where we were. For us it was becoming normal.'

This is the logic of war: the absurd becomes ordinary.

'We stayed on the pitch,' continues Mushfiq, 'because that was where we were supposed to be. You can lose your life during a war and we were prepared to face anything that might happen in a conflict. Our stadium was also close to the soldiers' quarters so we learned to live as footballers in the same conditions the combat soldiers lived in.'

Many Qarabag players wanted to join the troops fighting on the front line against the Armenian militia to defend Agdam, especially after what happened in Khojaly.

Mushfiq said, 'We would go to Commander Asif Maharammov, who everyone knew as Fred Asif, to tell him we wanted to fight, but he would answer, "I can find 11 soldiers easily, but I can't find 11 footballers. Your job is to play football to give hope to our people."'

Wednesday, 12 May 1993, a date that remains branded on the history of Qarabag and the whole of Azerbaijan. Qarabag took to the pitch at the Imaret Stadium to play Turan-Tovuz in the first leg of the Azerbaijan Cup semi-final. News reports estimated the attendance at around 8,000, ready to get behind the Horsemen, as the club is known – both for the Karabakh breed of horse and the two horses on its crest. Qarabag won 1-0 thanks to a goal from Yashar Huseynov. It was to be the last match played at the Imaret Stadium.

Mushfiq told me about it from his perspective, 'It was a great game. I remember the moment I got the ball and passed it to my brother who scored. I've never forgotten that moment. It was incredible. My pass and Yashar's goal. No one could have imagined that would be the last game we would play in Agdam.'

'I'm sad and disappointed,' remembers Yashar, 'to think that was the last goal I had the chance to score at the Imaret, in Agdam.'

That same day, the voice of Commander Allahverdi Bagirov rang out over the radio, 'Anyone who wants to drink cold water from the well has to come now!' Battalion 845 took the mountain village of Nakhichevanik, in Askeran province.

'According to AFFA regulations at that time,' explains Elshad Khudadatov, 'the final league semi-finals, for which we'd qualified, had to be played in Baku and Sumgait.'

Qarabag also won the second leg of the semi-final against Turan-Tovuz, 2-1, and qualified for the final of the Azerbaijan Cup at the Respublika Stadionu in Baku on 28 May 1993. Qarabag picked up the trophy, 1-0 winners over Inshaatchi Sabirabad – a team representing construction workers – thanks to a goal scored in the seventh minute of extra time by Mushfiq Huseynov.

Below is the score sheet for the Azerbaijan Cup won by Qarabag, the first since independence in 1993.

> FK Qarabag Agdam-Inshaatchi Sabirabad 1-0 (a.e.t.)
> Respublika Stadionu, Baku, Azerbaijan, 28 May 1993
> Scorer: Mushfiq Huseynov (97).

> *FK Qarabag Agdam:* Jamaleddin Aliyev, Settar Aliyev, Elshad Ahmadov, Aslan Kerimov, Zaur Garayev, Mahir Aliyev (Mammed Mammedov 113), Mehman Alishanov, Yashar Huseynov, Tabriz Hasanov (Elvariz Isayev 108), Mushfiq

Huseynov, Elshad Khudadatov. Manager: Aghasalim Mirjavadov

Inshaatchi Sabirabad: Vladimir Kopeykin, Ilgar Ibishov, Fikret Hasanov, Eldar Kerimov, Vadar Nuriyev, Serafat Aliyev, Natiq Rzayev (Rovshan Agayev 60/Mushfiq Aliyev 100), Ali Abushov, Yalcin Aliyev, Elmir Khankishiyev, Rafiq Hasanov.

* * *

Five days before the fall of Agdam, on 18 July 1993, Qarabag took to the pitch, still in Baku, against Turan-Tovuz for the Top League play-off semi-final. Once again, as in the cup semi-final, the Horsemen won 1-0, with a goal from Yashar Huseynov, this time scored in the 12th minute of extra time.

The Armenian militia entered the city after a six-week-long siege and took it, forcing tens of thousands of people into exile. The Qarabag players were not made aware of the terrible news straight away.

On 1 August, the team trained by Aghasalim Mirjavadov returned to the pitch at Baku's Respublika Stadionu.

They faced Khazar Sumgayit in the 1993 Azerbaijan Top League play-off final, the team from Agdam's greatest achievement, little more than a week after Agdam had ceased to exist, wiped out by hatred and the absurd destructive logic of war.

Qarabag won.

Here again is the score sheet for that historic final:

Qarabag FK Agdam-Khazar Sumgayit 1-0
Respublika Stadionu, Baku, Azerbaijan, 1
August 1993
Scorer: Yashar Huseynov (36)

FK Qarabag Agdam: Jamaleddin Aliyev, Settar
Aliyev, Elshad Ahmadov, Aslan Kerimov, Zaur
Garayev, Mahir Aliyev, Elvariz Isayev, Yashar
Huseynov, Tabriz Hasanov, Mushfiq Huseynov,
Elshad Khudadatov (Mammed Mammedov
88). Manager: Aghasalim Mirjavadov

Khazar Sumgayit: R. Salamov, V. Ismayilov,
A. Seferov (S. Rahimov 67), A. Mutallimov,
T. Nurmatov, K. Guliyev, I. Mammadov, M.
Orucov, A. Mammadov (Z. Asgerov 46), N.
Aliyev, A. Isayev.

9

The end is a new beginning

'IN 1993, we won the Azerbaijan league, the Azerbaijan Cup and automatically the Super Cup, leaving an indelible mark on the history of our country,' says the captain Sattar Aliyev. 'I was the first captain in Azerbaijani football to lift three trophies in the same year. During the final, the announcer at the stadium in Baku told us that Agdam had been occupied. We couldn't hold back the tears during the game.

'It wasn't the time to be happy. How can you celebrate winning a trophy if you've lost everything you have? We'd lost our Karabakh. I've never heard of anything like that happening anywhere in the world,' says Shahid Hasanov. 'You're playing football but at the same time you're losing your land, your family and everything you have. We played and suffered in the name of Qarabag and for our people.'

'It's really hard for me to express how I feel about my city in words, where I was born and where I grew up. I miss it every day. More than anything, I miss the birdsong

I would hear in the mornings when I woke up. Even today, sometimes I get out of bed and listen for that song, the same song I'd hear when I was a child,' remembers an emotional Mushfiq Huseynov.

'We won lots of titles that year, but every moment we were thinking about our city, our homeland,' Yashar Huseynov tells me. 'We had lost everything.'

Qarabag began their long exile, which has still not come to an end. The team has not played in Agdam since 12 May 1993, not a single home game. Over the years, the club has become the symbol and point of reference for hundreds of thousands of refugees forced to flee their homes during the war.

The Agdam team's new, temporary home became the Tofiq Ismayilov Stadium in Baku, a Neftchi facility, offered to provide a home to a team that had lost theirs because of the war. It was a facility that bore the name of a victim of the conflict, the secretary of state who had lost his life, along with 21 others, when the helicopter in which he was travelling was shot down above Karakend on 20 November 1991. Another of the victims, Public Prosecutor General Ismat Gayibov, had also given his name to one of Baku's stadiums, the long-standing home of Neftchi, prior to the construction of the Bakcell Arena.

But over the years that followed, Qarabag would play most of their home games on the pitch at Baku's Tofiq Bahramov Stadium, as it has been called since 1993. Known to everyone as the Respublika Stadionu, the stadium had initially been named after Stalin, then Lenin (during the USSR's De-Stalinization phase), prior to the fall of the Soviet Union.

The person after whom the main stadium of the Azerbaijani capital, the usual home of the national side, is named deserves some further consideration.

Let's go back a few decades to 1966, the year associated unequivocally in the history of football with the England World Cup. The most famous sport in the world, the magnificent game, came home, to the country that had laid down its rules and given it to the world. The 1966 World Cup Final was won 4-2 by the hosts after a period of extra time that followed the regulation 90 minutes, which had ended with England and West Germany locked at 2-2. In the 101st minute, England's Geoff Hurst picked up a cross from the right delivered by Alan Ball. From just outside the box, the striker fired a right-footed shot against the crossbar of Hans Tilkowski's goal, only for it to bounce on the ground before being cleared over the bar by the German defence. The linesman Tofiq Bahramov signalled to the Swiss referee Gottfried Dienst that the ball had crossed the line as it bounced, awarding the goal, and with it the eventual title of world champions, to England. Hurst's goal has gone down in footballing history as the ultimate 'ghost goal'.

The words 'Soviet Union' appear next to the name Tofiq Bahramov on the score sheet for that final, played on 30 June 1966 at Wembley in front of almost 97,000 spectators. From that day on, England fans have always thanked the linesman, referring to him as Russian. Bahramov was actually born on 29 January 1926 in Baku, the then Soviet Socialist Republic of Azerbaijan. After serving in the Red Army during the Second World War, Bahramov attempted a career as a footballer on his return to his homeland, but was forced to take a different path following a serious leg injury. He then decided to pursue a career in refereeing, taking charge of his first international match in 1964.

Bahramov was sent by the Soviet federation to the 1966 World Cup, where he refereed the Spain-Switzerland group game, which ended 2-1 after he disallowed a legitimate equaliser from the Swiss.

This, at the very least questionable debut, was surprisingly followed by the appointment of Bahramov, alongside his Czechoslovakian colleague Karol Galba (who had refereed the Uruguay v France, which ended in an uneventful 2-1 win for the South Americans during the group stage), to assist the Swiss referee Gottfried Dienst in the final – it was customary for referees to be used as linesmen at that time.

Bahramov became a national hero and went on to hold positions within the Azerbaijan Football Federation, both as an administrator in charge of appointing referees and general secretary. His fame was such that, after his death on 26 March 1993, the national stadium in the capital was renamed after him, the Republic Stadium that had previously borne the names of Stalin and Lenin.

But there was also a legend about Bahramov. Rumour had it that whenever he was asked how he could be so certain that the ball struck by Hurst really had crossed the goal line, he would reply, 'Stalingrad!' recalling the bloody Second World War battle between Germany and Russia. Italian sports journalist Gianni Brera was not alone in raising suspicions about the Azerbaijani referee's decision, arguing that Bahramov wanted somehow to avenge the Soviet Union's defeat at the hands of West Germany in the semi-final. In that game, the Italian referee Concetto Lo Bello had sent off striker Igor Chislenko when the Soviets were already down to ten men following Yozhef Sabo's injury; the final score was 2-1 to the West Germans, with the Soviets claiming the match had been stolen from them.

Robert Vergne, the French correspondent for *L'Équipe*, also failed to pull any punches, 'Germany displayed the worst football of this World Cup against the USSR. Those who talk of a plot in favour of the Germans and the English can support this theory with figures. In the last three games, Germany played against teams of either nine or ten players: ten-man Argentina (one sending off), nine-man Uruguay (two sendings off) and nine-man USSR (one serious injury; one sending off).'

On 13 October 2004, before the 2006 World Cup qualifying game between Azerbaijan and England (which ended with a 1-0 win for England), an imposing statue of Tofiq Bahramov was unveiled outside the stadium bearing his name. The referee has been immortalised just as he is about to blow the whistle, pointing with his right hand as if towards the pitch. According to the World Football Statue Database, the statue of Bahramov is the only one of a referee anywhere in the world. The job of unveiling the sculpture was given to Sepp Blatter and none other than Sir Geoff Hurst, who had benefited from the Azerbaijani linesman's decision 38 years earlier.

10

The ceasefire and the never-ending war

IN WRITING this book – for which I've tried to gather as much documentary material and direct evidence as possible, precisely to avoid appearing biased or running the risk of only telling a partial version of the facts – I had the great privilege of discussing the question of Nagorno-Karabakh with Mario Raffaelli.

Born in Trento on 15 May 1946 and elected to the Italian parliament for the first time in 1979 from the ranks of the Socialist Party, Mario Raffaelli has a truly exceptional CV in world diplomacy. Four times, between 1983 and 1989, he held the post of undersecretary for foreign affairs in the first and second Craxi governments and the cabinets headed by Goria and De Mita. His greatest diplomatic achievements include the successful conclusion of the negotiations that led to the signing of the Rome General Peace Accords between the government of Mozambique and RENAMO in the early 1990s. This agreement brought an end to a civil war that had, since

1981, been responsible for approximately one million deaths, of which an estimated 95 per cent were civilians.

On 24 March 1992, the then CSCE (now the Organization for Security and Co-operation in Europe OSCE), the Conference on Security and Cooperation in Europe, met in Helsinki for an additional session to request the organisation of an international peace conference to resolve the Nagorno-Karabakh conflict. Aimed at bringing the group of countries involved in negotiations between the warring parties together around a table to sign an agreement that would put an end to the hostilities – solving the geopolitical and ethnic dilemma and ending years of massacres – the conference was to be held in Minsk and has subsequently been referred to as the Minsk Group. I have used the phrase 'was to be held' in reference to the intended location because no one has yet sat down in Minsk; I have not, however, used the past tense to refer to the Minsk Group, as it is still active. More on paper than in fact.

Leadership of the Minsk Group was assigned to the Italian Mario Raffaelli, with whom I discussed the war at length, its unresolved issues, negotiations and prospects.

How did your involvement in the Nagorno-Karabakh conflict come about?

The CSCE had recently been formed and this was its first attempt to manage a conflict. Our aim was to agree a reconciliation conference with the parties and a chair had to be appointed on behalf of the CSCE in order to do so. Italy was chosen over two other candidates: France was rejected because it was considered too involved on the

Armenian side, given the large numbers of Armenians in the country; England was also rejected because of its historical relationship with Azerbaijan. Since the other candidates weren't considered neutral, Italy was selected as chair and I was chosen because I had relevant experience in Mozambique, where I'd coordinated a team of mediators within the Community of Sant'Egidio for peace in the African country.

How did your responsibilities evolve?
My work as head of the Minsk Group, which is now chaired by the Troika, lasted for about a year and a half, from April 1992 to September 1993. We succeeded in negotiating the ceasefire that is, essentially, still in force. My role became clearer during a series of meetings at the Villa Madama in Rome, in which Azerbaijan and Armenia participated, along with other representatives on behalf of the CSCE, including Turkey, the United States, Russia and France.

I was also involved in a series of field visits, not just to Azerbaijan and Armenia, but also to the countries with the greatest interest in the events, such as Iran and Russia. I was the first international representative to go to Stepanakert, in the self-proclaimed Nagorno-Karabakh Republic. During my mission, I only communicated with one president on the Armenian side, Levon Ter-Petrosyan, compared to three different presidents on the Azerbaijani side. The last of these was Heydar Aliyev, father of the current president, preceded by Abulfaz Elchibey and, for a very short period, Isa Gambar, for just one visit. I made several trips to the area affected by the conflict and had a great many opportunities because the presidency of the Minsk Group was properly supported, even logistically, allowing me to carry out a number of missions. On the one hand, I had plenty of opportunity to spend time in the area. On the other, in Italy we were trying to establish a dialogue with the parties and between the parties, which was complicated by the fact that the presence of Karabatsi representatives was not accepted by the Azerbaijani side.

* * *

On Thursday, 28 May 1992, *Corriere della Sera* reported, 'On the question of the Caucasian front, the Italian undersecretary for foreign affairs, Mario Raffaelli, chair of the "Minsk Conference" on Nagorno-Karabakh within the CSCE (Conference for Security and Cooperation in Europe), yesterday invited the participating states to a meeting in Rome on Monday. The conference is named after the capital of Belarus, its originally intended location. Armenia, Azerbaijan, Italy, USA, Russia, France, Germany, Sweden, Turkey, Czechoslovakia and Belarus will all be taking part.

'Raffaelli hopes that "negotiations will get off to a concrete start as quickly as possible to give substance to the peace process", and also stated that "the convening of this meeting, as well as the hoped-for possibility of sending CSCE observers to the areas of conflict are also significant developments".

'Representatives of the Armenian and Azerbaijani communities of Nagorno-Karabakh have also been invited to the Rome meeting "as observers".'

* * *

How did you resolve the stalemate?

With a series of balancing acts typical of diplomacy, we defined the two delegations from the self-proclaimed Nagorno-Karabakh Republic and, on the other side, the Azeris residing in those same territories as interested parties, without giving them any formal status. The compromise, in short, was that these so-called interested parties would not participate in the formal meetings, but only in the informal part, which was actually more significant. They both had the right to speak and, although it was difficult, this mechanism meant that the parties could finally talk to each other.

There was a slight difference in tone between the Armenians from Nagorno-Karabakh, who were very rigid, and Ter-Petrosyan, who was more open. I made an initial attempt to go to Stepanakert, but was frustrated by the attacks that were bordering on Agdam. A ceasefire had been agreed to allow me to go to the Karabatsi stronghold, to their capital, but it was violated and I was prevented from going. I had to take refuge in an armoured and protected basement in Agdam because the city was being bombed.

* * *

La Stampa, on 10 May 1992, had written: 'At the same time, the CSCE representative, the Italian ambassador Mario Raffaelli, arrived in Baku from Tehran and made an unsuccessful attempt to reach Karabakh. As a result of fierce fighting, Raffaelli's delegation was trapped in the basement of a building for two hours by the bombing in

Agdam, site of the region's Azerbaijani forces command base. Raffaelli left yesterday for Yerevan, the Armenian capital, in an attempt to organise the international conference on Karabakh that the CSCE hopes to hold in Minsk.

In Tehran, President Mammadov told Raffaelli that Azerbaijan would be willing to agree to a representation of Armenians from Karabakh at the conference, but only if they were a part of the Azerbaijani delegation. Azerbaijan does not recognise the region's self-proclaimed independence. It is clear that the Armenians will not accept this solution, all the more so now, after gains on the ground.'

* * *

So, I agreed a second attempt with Aliyev, preceded by a visit I made to Agdam, which had been attacked by the Armenians. Then, I went to Stepanakert, in Georgian helicopters, to spend a day in discussion with the Karabatsi. At the heart of all that effort, as well as trying to stop hostilities and implement a ceasefire, lay my attempt to get both sides to discuss a possible solution, helped by my roots in Trentino-Alto Adige. It seemed as if there were just two alternatives: the internal autonomy proposed by the Azerbaijanis, which was rejected by their counterparts given the theoretically federal experiment of the Soviet Union, and the independence declared by the Armenians.

But I explained that there was a third way forward, an autonomy that would remain internal to Azerbaijan, but would also have international protection. This autonomy would depend not only on the benevolence of the central government, but be permanently guaranteed at an international level. It was a unique and original solution on which I'd worked in South Tyrol and could be exported, given that there were strong similarities.

So, in your opinion, could South Tyrol have been, or still be, taken as a model solution for resolving the Nagorno-Karabakh conflict?
Around the table, I explained that the Italians had never agreed that a separation could be reached in the South Tyrol affair. The matter had therefore ended up in the hands of the United Nations. The UN established that, in order to bring an end to the issue, Austria would need to grant some kind of freedom.

* * *

Let's take a step back and explain what happened in Alto Adige to shed light on the solution proposed by Mario – on behalf of the CSCE – to the parties involved in the conflict in an attempt to reach an agreement to bring an end to the Nagorno-Karabakh conflict.

On 5 September 1946, on the sidelines of the Paris Peace Conference – where the fate of Europe and the divisions of the spheres of influence by the victorious wartime Allied powers were being discussed – the Italian foreign minister Alcide De Gasperi and his Austrian counterpart Karl Gruber signed the so-called Paris Treaty to define the thorny question of the safeguarding of Trentino-Alto Adige's German-speaking minority.

The Paris Treaty was the result of a compromise found during the political and diplomatic negotiations within the Paris Peace Conference. The three parties involved, Austria, Italy and the South Tyrolean minority, had no choice but to let go of what they wanted most. Italy obtained limited territorial sovereignty on the basis of agreements undertaken within the treaty; Austria had to give up on its request to retake the territories in question; and the South Tyroleans were denied the right of self-determination.

In essence, the logic of the treaty was that, according to the victorious powers, the conflict concerning the German minority in Italy should not be resolved by redefining the borders, but by using the tool of autonomy.

Most of the diplomatic work was carried out by those responsible for British foreign policy, who interpreted the Paris Treaty as merely one part of the more general question of collaboration between Italy and Austria and European unification as a whole. Although it would take a long time to fully and successfully implement, the Paris Treaty proved to be up to its original aims, both when it came to the UN debate on Alto Adige in 1960 and 61 and on the occasion of the development of the second statute of autonomy in 1972, until the final agreement was reached in 1992.

It was reported in *La Repubblica* on 12 June, 'The 30-year dispute between Italy and Austria over South Tyrol comes to a definitive conclusion. "Peace" was ratified yesterday in Vienna with the delivery to the Italian embassy of the "freedom declaration", the document with which the Austrian government acknowledges that Italy, with the approval of the Alto Adige "package", guarantees autonomy to the German-speaking populations of South Tyrol. The Austrian Foreign Minister delivered the "freedom" document to the Italian ambassador Alessandro Quaroni, bringing an end to a complicated diplomatic wrangle ushered in at the UN by then foreign minister Bruno Kreisky in 1960.

'The South Tyrolean "package" contains 137 measures implemented by the Italian government for the protection of the German and Ladin-speaking population, and for the autonomy of the province of Bolzano. The most significant regulations concern the right to mother tongue schooling, bilingualism in public services, and ethnic representation of the various linguistic groups in public employment and social care (housing, services), based on census figures.'

* * *

And Ter-Petrosyan was not unhappy with your solution?
He was much more open, and still is. Before the most recent elections in Armenia, as head of one of the opposition parties, he proposed the return of the Armenian-occupied provinces outside the historical borders of Nagorno-Karabakh, including the Agdam region, to the control of Azerbaijan. But he won only three per cent of the vote. In 1992, we happened to be in Helsinki for our annual meeting with the presidents and prime ministers of the CSCE just a few months after the ratification of the freedom clause by Austria, whose president spoke at length about the benefits

of the agreement. During dinner, Ter-Petrosyan turned to me and said, 'You weren't lying then!' after seeing his Austrian counterpart praise the solution I had put forward as being innovative and balanced for Karabakh.

Is this a decidedly anomalous conflict, given that after 25 years a genuine solution has yet to be found, apart from a ceasefire that is continuously violated? Why, still today, does Armenia refuse to recognise the independence of the Nagorno-Karabakh Republic?

Armenia has never recognised it because, if it did, it would be violating one of the fundamental rules of the CSCE, now the OSCE, to which it belongs. The anomaly is illustrated by the conflict between two principles, both extremely valid, which are the right to self-determination and the commitment only to change borders through consensus. The collision between these two principles has led, and still leads, to a stalemate, because neither can be embraced in situations of this kind. This is typical of conflicts in which it's hard to find a genuine solution, so an approach of self-containment has to be taken. The aim is to prevent the situation from igniting a wider conflict, an eventuality that, in this particular case, had, and still has, not inconsiderable potential. While the Karabakh question concerns what, all things considered, is a relatively small number of people, its geographical position means it could become the trigger for a much wider conflict. The primary objective is to prevent an escalation.

The role of context is therefore decisive in arriving at a shared solution.

A conflict can never be resolved unless there is a favourable environment, at least at a regional level, a context in which the countries involved are motivated by a sincere intent to find a solution. Then it becomes relatively easy to settle the differences between the opposing sides. If one or more powers, within the regional context, has different interests, things become much more complicated. In the Karabakh question, Russia, the largest power in the region, isn't interested in a stable solution, but wants to play a role in favour of either side, depending on the moment, to maintain its very strong military presence in the area and to be able to continue supplying arms to both warring parties. Although the Azerbaijani population is, in fact, an Iranian minority, it suits Iran for the situation to remain tense. Turkey is in secular conflict with Armenia for other reasons: without going into detail, there is a rather tangled international context and this greatly complicates the prospect of a stable and lasting peace.

Does that mean the ruling class of the parties involved needs to change?

More than anything, an option for stabilisation needs to emerge among the leadership of the countries involved. There is no doubt that if the groups in leadership fail to focus on stability, a lasting solution is absolutely impossible. There must be an interest among those in charge, who have a decisive role to play in tipping the balance one way or the other.

How do you view the self-proclaimed Nagorno-Karabakh Republic?

It may have been created as an entity, but it doesn't have a future that can lead to a recognised independence. In fact, everyone knows that on the day when an agreement is reached with Azerbaijan, annexation to Armenia would be an immediate consequence. It wouldn't lead to the birth of a real state. Nobody cares, not even the Armenians – demonstrated, as we've already said, by the fact that Armenia hasn't even recognised its independence.

In general, what are your memories of what you saw with your own eyes during the months of the conflict, on the ground?

The clashes in this war have always resulted in a relatively low number of victims that cannot be compared to other conflicts. What I did see, however, was that these clashes were of an unusual ferocity. Whenever there's an ideological, religious or ethnic component, the level of aggression tends to increase.

What is the current role of the Minsk Group, formed in 1992 and still active in resolving the conflict?

One of the big differences I see between yesterday and today is that Italy used to be responsible for leading the mediation. Because it wasn't directly involved in the situation, it was free to take positions that could go against one or other of the interested parties. People often think a mediator is someone who pretends to both sides that everything's going well, when, in fact, it's the opposite! A good mediator has to be prepared to take it in turns to disappoint both parties, otherwise they're not a mediator. To do this, of course, they can't be influenced by any interests.

Italy had the advantage of being a unique interest-free chair and, as such, was free to manoeuvre. Now, the Troika includes one of the big, if not leading, players in the conflict, Russia, which was inclined to implement its own policy in the area even then. Back then there was Vladimir Kazimirov – who I spoke with in Portuguese, given his diplomatic experience in Angola – who already tended to go his own way, but could be brought back into a unitary framework. It now seems that Russia wants its own way and the United States doesn't have a lot of influence.

Do you think there's any chance that Agdam and its region will return to Azerbaijan? Are President Aliyev's continued claims in this respect propaganda or a genuine political plan?
The stalemate and its ongoing nature depend precisely on this: some situations won't be resolved unless there's a body blow, which can't come from either of the interested parties without the creation of a broader context. On the one hand, it's unthinkable that Azerbaijan would agree to any solution involving the cession of part of its territory, especially if it's a question of areas that don't belong to the historical region of Karabakh. On the other, a return to the pre-conflict situation is also unthinkable, as is clear from Ter-Petrosyan's recent result.

The difference, compared to a few years ago, is that previously there was no comparison from a military perspective; Armenia had clear supremacy. But today, by virtue of oil resources and their conversion into arms, Azerbaijan is in a very different place. There's also been another consequence of this rebalancing of strength on the ground: in one respect, it's another factor that could lead to a hypothetical solution, but it could also be the fuse that triggers a conflict with unpredictable consequences.

* * *

Every year since 2006, the Global Firepower website has drawn up a ranking of the most powerful armies in the world, using more than 55 factors to determine the Power Index assigned to each nation. Its 2018 ranking had Azerbaijan in 53rd position, while Armenia was in 84th. The Azerbaijani army is by far the strongest in the region, with Georgia in 82nd place in the ranking.

* * *

Did you ever feel as if there was a genuine risk of escalation during your mandate?
In my opinion, it's more likely now than in 1992–93, precisely because of the imbalance in terms of military strength at the time. Also, back then, there was no risk of the situation getting out of hand given the international context.

When I think about a possible escalation, I don't think about a preordained plan, but more about the prospect that the situation could get out of hand due to this new balance of forces and because, for better or for worse, Russia is now unpredictable.

What role can the European Union play?
It could, in theory, play a role, in this as in other contexts; in Nagorno-Karabakh more than elsewhere, as it's a neighbouring area. The problem is that to have a role, Europe must first exist. But Europe can only start to exist if it begins to play a role in these contexts. It's a vicious circle.

* * *

Mario Raffaelli's work in Nagorno-Karabakh produced several reports that formed the basis of four UN resolutions:

- Resolution 822 (1993), 30 April 1993:
  Demands the cessation of hostilities with
  a view to establishing a ceasefire and the
  withdrawal of all occupying forces from the
  Kelbajar district and other areas recently
  occupied by Armenia. It also urges the
  resumption of negotiations within the
  framework of the Minsk Group peace
  process.

- Resolution 853 (1993), 29 July 1993:
  Demands the cessation of hostilities and the
  withdrawal of occupying troops from the
  province of Agdam and other occupied areas
  of Azerbaijan.

- Resolution 874 (1993), 14 October 1993:
  Calls for an effective and permanent ceasefire
  established with the help of the Government
  of the Russian Federation in support of

the Minsk Group and implementation of
Security Council resolutions 822 and 853.

- Resolution 884 (1993), 12 November 1993:
  Calls for the resumption of the ceasefire and
  the withdrawal of occupying forces from the
  Zangelan district and the city of Goradiz,
  and other occupied areas.

Overall, it is clear that there was a demand for the
withdrawal of Armenian and Karabatsi militia from
the occupied territories of Azerbaijan. One resolution
specifically concerned Agdam.

The culmination of the work carried out by the
Minsk Group was the agreement signed on 5 May 1994
in Bishkek, the capital of Kyrgyzstan, which has, in fact,
frozen the conflict until the war for taking back Adgam
started in 2020.

* * *

Bishkek, 5 May 1994

Participants of the meeting held in May
4-5 in Bishkek on the initiative of the CIS
InterParliamentary Assembly, Parliament of the
Kyrgyz Republic, Federal Congress and Ministry
of Foreign Affairs of the Russian Federation:

express determination to assist in all possible
ways to the cessation of armed conflict in and
around Nagorno-Karabakh, which does not
only cause irretrievable losses to Azerbaijani and
Armenian people, but also significantly affects

the interests of other countries in the region and seriously complicates the international situation;

supporting the April 15, 1994 Statement by the CIS Council of heads of states, express readiness to fully support the efforts by heads and representatives of executive power on cessation of the armed conflict and liquidation of its consequences by reaching an appropriate agreement as soon as possible;

advocate a naturally active role of the Commonwealth and Inter-Parliamentary Assembly in cessation of the conflict, in realisation of thereupon principles, goals and the UN and OSCE certain decisions (first of all the UN Security Council resolutions 822, 853, 874, 884);

call upon the conflicting sides to come to common senses: cease to fire at the midnight of May 8 to 9, guided by the February 18, 1994 Protocol (including the part on allocating observers), and work intensively to confirm this as soon as possible by signing a reliable, legally binding agreement envisaging a mechanism, ensuring the non-resumption of military and hostile activities, withdrawal of troops from occupied territories and restoration of communication, return of refugees;

agree to suggest Parliaments of the CIS member-states to discuss the initiative by Chairman of

Council of the Inter-Parliamentary Assembly V. Shumeyko and Head of the Assembly's Peacemaking Group on Nagorno-Karabakh M. Sherimkulov on creating a CIS peacemaking force;

consider appropriate to continue such meetings for peaceful resolution of the armed conflict;

express gratitude to the people and leadership of Kyrgyzstan for creating excellent working conditions, cordiality and hospitality.

ON BEHALF OF DELEGATIONS:
A. Jalilov (signed by R. Guliyev, Chairman of the Azerbaijani Supreme Soviet)
K. Babourian (Chairman of the Nagorno-Karabakh Republic Supreme Soviet)
B. Ararktsian (Chairman of the Supreme Soviet of Armenia)
V. Shumeyko (Chairman of the Council of Federation of Russia)
M. Sherimkulov (Chairman of the Supreme Soviet of Kyrgyzstan)
V. Kazimirov (Plenipotentiary Representative of the President of the Russian Federation, Head of the Russian Mediation Mission)
M. Krotov (Head of the Secretariat of the Council of the Inter-Parliamentary Assembly of member states)

This is the culmination of a never-ending war. A frozen conflict, which it is not in the interest of any of the contenders to definitively conclude. Better to continue to be able to exploit it politically, as propaganda, or to scare others away.

Or to continue to sell weapons.

* * *

Baku, 23 November 2017
44, Kichic Gala Kuchesi (Icheri Sheher)
Italian Embassy

'Football also has a strong political significance for Azerbaijan. Being in the Champions League and bringing international attention to the Karabakh issue seems like a dream come true for them. Tomorrow will also see the holding of an important summit in Brussels between the heads of state and governments of six of the so-called Eastern Partnership countries: Ukraine, Belarus, Moldova, Georgia, Armenia and Azerbaijan.'

This is the opinion of a man sitting in front of me on a sofa, Augusto Massari, the 46-year-old Italian ambassador to Azerbaijan, who has been in his post since 10 August 2017. The morning after Qarabag's 4-0 loss to Chelsea, he granted me a long interview.

'One of the topics on the table will be the Karabakh question, but it won't be easy to find a shared text for the final declaration, so the game has served to draw attention to this war that has been going on for 25 years. They call it a "frozen conflict", but it isn't frozen. There was a ceasefire, but the peace treaty was never signed. Plus, the agreements are continually violated, dozens of times in a single day.'

This is the list of so-called incidents between Armenians and Azerbaijanis in the area affected by the war following the ratification of the Bishkek protocol:

- Clashes in Karmiravan, 1999
- Clashes in Martakert, 2000
- Clashes in Fizuli, 2003
- Clashes in Agdam, 2005
- Clashes in Martakert, 2008
- Clashes in Martakert, 2010
- Clashes on the Armenia-Azerbaijan border, 2012
- Armenia-Azerbaijan clashes, 2014
- Armenia-Azerbaijan clashes, 2015

The Economist puts the number of victims of ceasefire violations at around 3,000. The figure should actually be considerably lower; both sides in the war deliberately include those who die in accidents in their death figures. Since 1994, however, there have been more than 7,000 violations of the ceasefire, 100 in 2015 alone.

On 4 April 2016, *Il Fatto Quotidiano* reported, 'In the last few hours, as a result of the Azeri army's retaliations, up to 170 soldiers have been killed and 12 enemy armoured vehicles destroyed, said the Azerbaijan Ministry of Defence. According to official sources, Armenian troops panicked, abandoning weapons and ammunition after being overwhelmed by Azerbaijani units. Meanwhile, the Baku army suffered heavy losses in an attempt to break the lines of Nagorno-Karabakh, whose militia destroyed five tanks and killed 25 soldiers.

'Clashes have intensified since 1 April, namely since the death of Vladimir Melkonian, 20, a soldier from the self-proclaimed republic. This was followed by reciprocal attacks and accusations. The Armenians claim to have shot down an enemy helicopter; Yerevan points the finger at Baku for having launched a general offensive with the use of artillery, tanks and aviation. This was followed by the unilateral truce declared by Azerbaijan, which Armenia does not support. A situation in which Turkey sides with Baku.

'Erdogan is convinced that the disputed territory "will undoubtedly one day return to its legitimate master, Azerbaijan". But Yerevan has warned Istanbul not to meddle. Georgia sees a ceasefire on the horizon, but the tension in the area has also required the diplomatic intervention of the country that has often played the role of mediator and arbiter: Russia, which sells arms to both Armenia and Azerbaijan. Leader of the Kremlin, Vladimir Putin, has asked "the warring parties to cease hostilities immediately."'

A never-ending war, as Ambassador Massari calls it: the clearest proof came in the night between 1 and 2 April 2016, when Azerbaijani troops launched an attack along almost the entire line of contact with the self-proclaimed Nagorno-Karabakh Republic. The attack surprised the Armenians, who were concerned that the Azerbaijani army might reach as far as Stepanakert. This was followed by bombings, ground attacks, feverish international talks and calls to bring an end to the hostilities that were resulting in numerous deaths. When the Armenian defences managed to reorganise, blocking the Azerbaijanis' route, they left dozens of soldiers on the field. On 5 April, on the initiative of the Russians, it was agreed that a ceasefire would come into force at noon that same day.

Azerbaijan celebrated the reconquest of 2,000 hectares of its territory usurped by the Karabatsi; the defeated Armenians recognised that they had lost only 800 hectares.

An interesting analysis that appeared on the Pravda. ru website at the time describes how the situation has changed between the forces on the ground – as had already been explained by Mario Raffaelli – leading to military action by Azerbaijan.

The article reads, 'The main initiator of hostilities is, of course, Azerbaijan. The country's administration assumed that the time had come. "Time is on our side," Karen Mirzoyan, foreign minister of Nagorno-Karabakh, told Bloomberg. "The more time passes, the more successful we are in strengthening our statehood and the closer we move to the international recognition of our independence," the official said.

'Secondly, the economy of Azerbaijan has shown significant growth during recent years. The country has acquired a variety of weapons. Azerbaijan's military spending has increased 30 times over the last decade and amounted to 4.8 billion dollars in 2015. This is larger than the entire state budget of Armenia, Bloomberg wrote. This is what they call vanity of a more successful and wealthier state.

'Thirdly, the international situation has changed dramatically. Russia, the guarantor of Armenia's security, is now in a difficult position. The last thing that Russia needs now is another bloody conflict near its borders – the Syrian and Ukrainian crises are more than just costly. The Russian economy still remains under the burden of western sanctions, global oil prices and large-scale projects, such as the construction of the Kerch bridge (from mainland Russia to Crimea) and the FIFA World Cup that Russia is hosting in 2018.'

11

From that muffled scream to the bright lights of the Champions League

AFTER THEIR historic first league win in 1993, which was tinged with sadness, Qarabag failed to cement their position as champions of Azerbaijan the following season, losing out to Turan Tovuz by just one point. Finishing as runners-up in 1994/95, they ended the 1995/96 season in fourth place.

'There's one story that neither I nor Arthur have been able to get to the bottom of,' Thomas Goltz tells me, adding, 'but I think you might be able to shed some light on it.'

'What's it about?' I ask, my curiosity piqued.

'I still clearly remember the TV pictures from that afternoon. Qarabag secured a 3-0 home win and the stadium announcer shouted, "Qarabag champions!" The celebrations started on the pitch, but the atmosphere changed a couple of minutes later. A smartly dressed man appeared and said something. An icy chill came down and lots of the Qarabag players put their heads in their hands and started crying.'

I take up the challenge and start investigating.

The season in question was 1996/97; the Yüksək dəstə roll of honour for Azerbaijan football's top flight shows Neftchi Baku in first place. The top of the final table reads:

Pos. Teams	Pts	PL	W	D	L	GS	GA	GD
1. PFC Neftchi Baku	74	30	23	5	2	98	20	+78
2. Qarabag Agdam	71	30	23	2	5	61	25	+36
3. Khazri Buzovna	66	30	20	6	4	59	23	+36

Neftchi were champions with 74 points (three points for a win), with Qarabag three behind.

So, what were the images of celebration seen by Thomas Goltz and published as special content on the DVD of his 2015 film dedicated to the club, *On Aggregate: Champions Without a Home*? I couldn't close this page in the story without resolving the dilemma that was shaping up to be increasingly odd and compelling.

A photo – given to me by Nurlan Ibrahimov, the Qarabag press officer – convinced me once and for all of the uniqueness of the story and that I should thoroughly investigate what took place that year, when Goltz believed the title was stolen from the team exiled from Agdam.

This is what happened.

Sunday, 1 June 1997, the 30th and final game of the season; Qarabag beat Shamkir 3-0 and Neftchi win 2-1 away at Polis Akademy Baku. The team from Agdam, the city that no longer exists, pose on the pitch to celebrate their second title: the Cyrillic characters that make up the words 'гарабаг чемпион' (Qarabag Champions) jump out unmistakably on the stadium screen behind the players.

But the title fails to appear on the roll of honour and the players present that day seem to have erased what happened from their memories. As if the league was never played that year. Why?

I find the answer to what happened in an AzPFL (Azərbaycan Peşəkar Futbol Liqası, the Azerbaijan professional league) document reproduced below:

Yüksək dəstə - 1996/97
(AFFA-nın əsasnaməsinə uyğun, UEFA-nın tanımadığı cədvəl)

		əsas komanda	U15	U16	bonus	cəmi
1.	Qarabağ (Ağdam)	71	15	15	15	86
2.	Neftçi (Bakı)	74	13	8	10,5	84,5
3.	Xəzri (Buzovna)	66	14	13	13,5	79,5
4.	Turan (Tovuz)	64	5	7	6	70
5.	Sumqayıt	58	10	14	12	70
6.	Kəpəz (Gəncə)	58	12	12	12	70
7.	Fərid (Bakı)	47	0	11	5,5	52,5
8.	Pambıqçı (Bərdə)	38	9	10	9,5	47,5
9.	Viləş (Masallı)	33	8	9	8,5	41,5
10.	Bakı fəhləsi	37	0	5	2,5	39,5
11.	Kür-Nur (Mingəçevir)	25	11	0	5,5	30,5
12.	OİK (Bakı)	27	6	0	3	30
13.	Şəmkir	26	0	6	3	29
14.	Polis Akademiyası (Bakı)	22	7	0	3,5	25,5
15.	Pambıqçı (Neftçala)	21	0	0	0	21
16.	Azərbaycan U-18	13	0	0	0	13

AFFA-nın əsasnaməsinə görə medallar uşaq komandaların çempionatının nəticələrinə əsasən verilən bonus xalların köməyi olmaqla müəyyənləşib. Hər yaş qrupunda 1-ci yer 15, 2-ci 14, 3-cü 13 ardıcıllığı ilə bonus alıb. 2 yaş qrupunda toplanan orta xal əsas komandaya əlavə olunub. UEFA bu cür çempionluğu tanımayıb.

Even with no knowledge of Azerbaijani, it's clear that Qarabag Agdam finished the season top of the table ahead of Neftchi that year. In the first column, Qarabag appear to have 71 points compared with Neftchi's 74. But it's also true that, in the final column on the right, the Huseynov brothers' team have 86 points, compared with 84 and a half for the oil workers' side.

The three lines of text under the table attempt to clarify what happened. During the 1996/97 season, the AFFA was experimenting with new league regulations in an attempt to promote the growth of youth football. It was decided that the domestic title would be assigned based not only on the results of the team that finished first, but that bonus points would be awarded proportional to the results achieved by the respective under-15 and under-16 teams. According to this criterion, Qarabag should have been the champions in 1996/97. UEFA, however, made it clear that it would not recognise the result, given that, according to international regulations, titles are awarded on the basis of first-team results only; Neftchi were therefore awarded their third domestic title from six since independence.

I had the chance to ask Elkhan Mammadov, the AFFA general secretary and member of various UEFA and FIFA committees, to explain this anomaly that affected so many Qarabag players.

'The season in question,' Mammadov told me, 'was the fourth since the setting up of the Azerbaijani football federation and the second since the AFFA's membership of UEFA and FIFA. At the time, a number of experimental methods were applied to the organisation of the domestic league and small errors were inevitable. To be honest, we don't believe this is the right way to determine the winner.

'AFFA is a member of UEFA and this membership brings with it certain commitments. Domestic league winners have the opportunity to compete in UEFA club competitions, so the AFFA has to follow UEFA rules in awarding the title of champions of Azerbaijan. Even if the system applied by the AFFA that season was not entirely correct, the main reason for the change was the desire to develop and improve competitiveness within football in the country and to increase interest in League B. Obviously, we don't believe that calculating club points in this way is correct.'

'Who does the AFFA think were champions of Azerbaijan in 1996/97? Neftchi or Qarabag?' I asked in conclusion.

'During the 1996/97 season, PFC Neftchi were more successful than the other clubs playing in the top flight and scored more points from their games, so we think it's right to consider Neftchi the winners.'

It was after narrowly missing out on that title that Qarabag's years of darkness began. With no stadium or city, forced to constantly seek hospitality at the capital's various grounds, and lacking solid investment, the club came one step away from bankruptcy.

In strictly footballing terms, however, those same years brought a number of significant results. In the 1996/97 season, Qarabag made their historic debut in European cup competition; in the previous season, Neftchi had beaten the team from Agdam 3-0 in the Azerbaijan Cup Final, but, by virtue of Neftchi also topping the league, a place in the Cup Winners' Cup was granted to Qarabag. On 8 August 1996, Qarabag Agdam took on the Finnish team MyPa Anjalankoski at Baku's Tofiq Bahramov Stadium.

The team fielded by manager Aghasalim Mirjavadov for the game was: Djamalladin Aliyev, Elshad Ahmadov, Aslan Kerimov (Yashar Huseynov 83), Tabriz Hasanov, Sattar Aliyev, Bakhtiyar Musayev (Emin Salmanov 46), Tarlan Ahmadov, Nazim Aliyev, Mirbagir Isayev, Mushfiq Huseynov, Mais Azimov.

Qarabag lost 1-0 due to a goal from the Finnish player Sami Mahlio seven minutes from time, but, thanks to Bakhtiyar Musayev in the 27th minute of the second leg at the Saviniemen Jalkapallostadion in Anjalankoski, on the end of a tentative goal kick from the keeper Jakonen, the two-legged tie went to extra time. However, just as the teams were preparing for penalties, in the 120th minute Mauri Keskitalo scored quickly from a cross lofted into the box from a free kick. Elimination stung, naturally, but the satisfaction of finally playing on the large and prestigious European stage was greater.

Shortly afterwards, at a time of great crisis behind the scenes at the club, Qarabag achieved one of the best results in their history. On 19 June 1999 at the Municipal Stadium in Rishon LeZion, in front of just over 1,200 spectators, a double from the reliable Mushfiq Huseynov gave Qarabag a 2-1 win over hosts Maccabi Haifa in the first round of the Intertoto Cup, making them the first team from Azerbaijan to win an away game in European competition.

During three difficult seasons, between 1998 and 2001, Qarabag finished fourth, eighth and, finally, ninth in the table. The end of a beautiful story appeared to be knocking at the door.

The club was saved thanks to its acquisition by the agri-food giant Azersun Holding, owned by the brothers Abdolbari and Hassan Gozal, Iranians from a Kurdish family who later moved to Turkey. It has often been both said and written that the Gozal family had (and still has) traditionally close links to the presidential Aliyev family.

In 2001, the club took the official name of Qarabag Azersun, only to return to its original name of Qarabag FK in 2004. Under Azersun management, a new era was ushered in for the Agdam team: the first two seasons under the leadership of manager Shahin Diniyev brought two third-place finishes; good results considering the team had come within a whisker of disappearing from football altogether, something sadly all too common in Azerbaijan.

In 2004/05, the management decided on a change of course and brought Igor Ponomarev to the touchline. An Olympic champion for the USSR in 1998, Ponomarev was the holder, as a player, of an unusual record: the most penalties scored consecutively in the Soviet top flight – no fewer than 24.

Ponomarev brought with him his 26-year-old son Anatoli, taken from Inter Baku, who had been raised in Swedish football and gained experience with Mallorca's B team, scoring nine goals in 15 games as a striker that season.

'We had a good team and good organisation at club level,' Anatoli tells me. 'In 2004, Qarabag decided to shift their focus more towards professional football, towards building a club that could compete at a high level, following a general process of growth in Azerbaijani football.'

In the final games of the season, following a series of negative results, Qarabag lost ground in the title race after being right up there.

'I think we were the best team that year. It was a shame we lost the title. My father was really sad we couldn't win it,' Anatoli remembers regretfully.

His words are echoed by Emrah Celikel, current director general of Qarabag, whose story at the club began that same season.

'I started working for Qarabag in 2004,' he says. 'I'd already been with Azersun Holding for 20 years by then and, one day, vice-president Tahir Gozal asked me to take care of the football team owned by the group. That was how I started as sporting director of Qarabag.'

'What were the club's plans at that time?' I ask him.

'At that time, vice-president Tahir Gozal's intention was to impregnate the club's whole system with his philosophy. We all had to obey his philosophy and try to do our best to be consistent with his ideas. Gozal wasn't interested in winning immediately, in obtaining immediate results, but in implementing a project that could guarantee a successful and stable future.'

'Was the choice of Ponomarev as manager part of this vision?'

'Igor was one of the most famous footballers in Azerbaijan and he had also managed the national side. A profile of that kind represented something new for a team like Qarabag.'

After the season with Ponomarev, in which Qarabag also returned to European competition after three years away from the continental stage, Boyukagha Aghayev was chosen as the next manager.

'We changed lots of players in 2005/06 and, under the new manager, we brought home the first trophy during our management: the Azerbaijan Cup,' says Celikel. 'It was an unexpected success, but it was a sign that Tahir Gozal had made us believe we had the chance to build a great Qarabag.'

The team from Agdam defeated Karvan 2-1 at Baku's Inter Arena (also known as the Shafa Stadium) in the final on 3 June 2006. The winning goal was scored by Samir Musayev three minutes from the end of the regulation 90.

The reins of the team passed to the Turk Rasim Kara, who had won the league title in 2005 at the helm of Khazar Lankaran. After a year and a half, his path and that of Qarabag diverged.

On the eve of the 2008/09 season came the key choice in the Agdam side's recent history. I'll let Celikel, who experienced it first-hand, tell the story. 'We all knew Gurban Gurbanov as a player,' he explains. 'He was one of the most talented in the history of Azerbaijan. He was only 33 when he began his coaching career at Neftchi. After Rasim Kara left the club, at our first meeting Gurbanov told us his only focus was on the players in the Qarabag squad and that he could make them work hard to get the best out of them. At the time, we were based at Ruslan 93, a sports centre on Heydar Aliyev Road in Baku as we didn't have a ground that was properly ours. I remember the first time we met there. Gurbanov didn't say much. He just asked us for a list of players that would be available to him and we immediately came to an initial agreement on a six-month contract. From that first moment, I believed he would achieve the best possible results with Qarabag. I thank God we made the right choice.'

'On a human level, what impression did Gurbanov make on you?'

'That of a very modest and humble person. He said we could work together and get the best out of ourselves together. Perhaps no one back then could believe that Qarabag would play in the Champions League group stages under Gurbanov, but already, from his initial impact, he exuded a strong positive energy. We had found a sincere person, both in his faith and personality.'

'There's a particular anecdote about Gurbanov's name. Do you want to tell me about it?'

'Tahir Gozal always used to say that a person with the same name and surname is sure to be a genuine person, a real man. Gozal and Gurbanov's philosophies came together wonderfully; the club believed in the manager's ideas, this was key to our relationship and to the growth of Qarabag.'

Despite these idyllic premises, Gurbanov's first season on the Qarabag bench failed to bring the team significant league results, although he did win the Azerbaijan Cup on his debut, beating Inter Baku 1-0 at the Tofiq Bahramov in the final with a goal scored by Vagif Javadov from the penalty spot.

'To be honest, it's never crossed our minds to replace Gurbanov,' explains the director. 'Gozal always tells us repeatedly, "He's our manager and we should never think about anyone else." We trust him and we believe in him. That's enough for us.'

What Gurbanov brought from the start of his time on the bench for the Agdam side, exiled to Baku, was a change in mentality: no more wild purchasing of foreign footballers, known in Azerbaijan as 'legionaries', and instead room for Azerbaijani footballers, drawing heavily on the club's youth ranks.

Victory in the Azerbaijan Cup allowed Qarabag to return to Europe and on 16 July 2009 they played in the first leg of the second qualifying round of the Europa League. Gurbanov's team found themselves in Tromsø, playing Rosenborg, 21-time Norwegian champions, with several Champions League appearances, including the quarter-finals of Europe's biggest club competition in 1996/97.

A real challenge on paper. The team asked to be able to observe a minute's silence before the start of the game to commemorate the victims of the city that no longer exists. UEFA's response was a firm no. Slovakian František Laurinec was a member of the UEFA Executive Committee at the time; I asked him why Qarabag's request was refused. 'UEFA's general policy is to avoid any kind of political message,' was his dry reply.

Qarabag went home with an incredible goalless draw that day, but the real apotheosis came a week later. On 23 July, the anniversary of the fall of Agdam, a feat no one would ever have expected was pulled off in front of 20,000 fans at Baku's Tofiq Bahramov Stadium. Or, at least, no one who knew the history of Qarabag and what had happened in Agdam. In the first minute of injury time at the end of the first half, Rashad Sadigov, a central defender in the number 14 shirt, slotted a free kick into the top corner from the edge of the area. Jubilation! Qarabag had knocked out the experienced Norwegians 26 years after the end of the city of Agdam, 5,844 days after the beginning of the exile. The beginning of an end that, on that summer evening, became the dawning of a new era. Qarabag's captain in the victory over Rosenborg was Aslan Kerimov, also on the field for that bittersweet win in the 1993 championship, one of the last heroes of the Imaret and the ideal figure to mark the transition between the two eras.

This was the victorious Qarabg team against Rosenborg at the Tofiq Bahramov Stadium on 23 July 2009: Ferhad Veliyev, Elnur Allahverdiyev, Rashad F. Sadigov, Admir Teli, Maksim Medvedev, Rashad E. Sadigov, Aslan Kerimov (captain) (Namik Yusifov 68), Elvin Mammadov (Zaur Hashimov 72), Ermin Imamaliyev (Rauf Aliyev 82), Vuqar Nadirov, Vagif Javadov. Manager: Gurban Gurbanov.

That was the day the whole of Europe became aware of the existence of Qarabag. Mainstream international media gradually began taking an interest in the unique events at the club, its city and its players, as they still do. Stories such as that of Vuqar Nadirov, a striker born in Agdam whose father, Ershad, died defending the city on the day it fell to the Armenians, and his uncle Adil, one of the key players in the club's rebirth in 1987. Or that of Qara Qarayev, born in the Armenian-occupied city of Fuzuli, who began his career at the age of 16 after being discovered by a talent scout while he was playing football on a rubble-strewn pitch in a field for refugees near the capital Baku. The midfielder Namiq Yusifov, born in

Saint Petersburg, who, after the death of his father, moved briefly to Agdam, to the house of his grandmother who urged him to flee to Baku before the Armenians razed the city to the ground. And then, the legendary (an adjective so often abused but one that really does apply in this case) Rashad Sadigov, 'Captain Sadigov', who took the armband from Aslan Kerimov, who left the club and retired from football in 2011.

Sadigov is a refugee, a displaced person, like the club's fans; his family originates from the province of Kelbajar, wedged between what was traditionally Karabakh and Armenia, occupied by the Armenians since April 1993. Rashad, born in 1982, has always been a fighter on the pitch, a true leader, someone who could easily have played in a higher league given his competitive and athletic qualities. During his career, he did, in fact, play in Iran's top flight, winning the league title in a Foolad shirt, and in Turkey's Süper Lig, for Kocaelispor and Eskişehirspor, before returning permanently to Qarabag in the summer of 2011, following an initial spell of a few months during the 2009/10 season.

At the end of his loan to Kocaelispor, where he had been a favourite with the fans, who had given him the nickname of 'Terminator', he returned home determined to sign a new contract with Neftchi. But the AFFA had set the deadline for the summer transfer window as 20 August that year and there were no exceptions, not even for a player like Rashad Sadigov, who had already won some 40 games for the Azerbaijani national side. Sadigov, convinced that the deadline was 31 August – as in the majority of European leagues – failed to obtain federation approval for the transfer. Top federation officials would have allowed him to play with the Neftchi reserve team in the second division, but Sadigov chose instead to keep up his fitness by playing basketball. He was picked up temporarily by the NTD BK team from Baku and played his first game in his new team and new sport against Khazar-BDU, who chalked up an impressive 105-53 win. Rashad scored 13 points in that game, but his performances on the court were not enough to convince the Azerbaijan football manager, Shahin Diniyev, who failed to call him up. He was missing for the first time in five years.

Over time, Rashad became Gurban Gurbanov's right-hand man, to the extent that he was the manager's voice and eyes on the pitch. But that was not all: the manager appointed Rashad coach of the Qarabag reserve team.

As far as the mainstream European and global media were concerned, Qarabag were the 'refugee club', and word began to spread as their results became more and more impressive. Until they eventually became incredible.

The adventure that began with knocking out Rosenborg failed to deliver a fairy-tale ending when, after getting through one more round at the expense of the Finnish team Honka, Qarabag were eliminated one step away from qualifying for the group stage. The team from Agdam were defeated in a decisive two-leg play-off against the Dutch side FC Twente – make a note of their name as they will soon reappear in this story, next time under completely different circumstances.

The 2008/09 season was characterised by one important change: for the last three games, Qarabag went back to play in the Agdam region. In January 2008, President Ilham Aliyev himself went to Guzanli – a village 40km north of the ghost city, in the same district, in an area not occupied during the conflict and under full control of the Azerbaijan government. There he inaugurated the so-called Agdam Olimpiya İdman Kompleksi, a large and modern multidisciplinary sports centre. Built on a three-hectare site and home to the Guzanli Olympic Complex Stadium, it included a 2,000-seater football stadium. The symbolism was significant for Qarabag when, in the spring of 2009, the club obtained permission to play their home games in Guzanli.

The game that marked the return of the team led by Gurban Gurbanov to their home region was played on 1 May 2009. In front of a stadium full of cheering fans, almost in disbelief at the opportunity to see their heroes play near Agdam once more, Qarabag drew 1-1 against Inter Baku, with the home team scoring, thanks to the Bosnian Sedat Şahin, and the team from the capital equalising through the Latvian Andrejs Rubins.

Qarabag played two more games in Guzanli before the end of the season: the last home game in the league, won 1-0 against Khazar Lankaran due to a goal from the Macedonian Artim Šakiri, and victory in the second leg of the Azerbaijan Cup semi-final over FC Baku.

* * *

Like a lion, you take to the pitch once more
You defeat your opponents in every game
We are your fans everywhere and always
Make us happy again with victory

Qarabag! Qarabag!
Qarabag, Qarabag you are the champions
You're like an uncompromising, unbeatable,
courageous woman
You score a lot of goals in every game
Our hearts are with you, we are proud of you!

You are the strongest of the strong,
You are the eye of our country
You decorate matches with your beautiful goals
Your name is linked to the homeland
You are the sultan of the clouds
Surprise Europe, Qarabag we are with you

Qarabag! Qarabag!
Qarabag, Qarabag you are the champions.

Qarabag Agdam FK fan chant

* * *

In 2010, Qarabag's European adventure again came to
an end, in the Europa League play-offs against Borussia
Dortmund, after winning three rounds at the expense of
opponents such as the Macedonians Metalurg Skopje,
the Northern Irish team Portadown and the Poles of
Wisła Kraków. But the project to build a winning club
was making progress.

'I chose Qarabag without giving it too much thought.
At the time I was playing in Ukraine and had my first
contact with them when they were looking for a left-
back, but I still had two years to run on my contract

with Kryvbas. I called my compatriot Admir Teli, who was at Qarabag at the time, and asked him about the team. Owing to involvement from the club, who managed to convince Kryvbas, despite me still being under contract, I was initially signed on loan for six months and left for Azerbaijan,' said Ansi Agolli, pillar of the Albanian national side and still the backbone of the Qarabag defence, the team he joined in the summer of 2010.

'I'd only been to Azerbaijan once before that, with the national team, and I didn't know much about Qarabag's situation. As soon as their people got in touch to find out how willing I would be to move, I immediately started searching online for any information I could find about the team, players, staff and city.'

The first impression left on someone who would go on to become a symbol of Qarabag was not the best. 'I got to Baku in late June and remember finding the weather too hot as soon as I got off the plane. But the pitch immediately gave me completely different impressions and answers,' Ansi tells me.

'The team had just come back from pre-season training in Ankara. Four days after I arrived in Baku, we played the first Europa League qualifying game against the Macedonian team Metalurg. The welcome my team-mates and the staff gave me was very warm. From the first encounter with my new supporters, during the game, I felt at home from the opening minutes. I realised right then that I'd made the right choice.'

During that summer, another high-quality foreign player joined the squad made up almost exclusively of

Azerbaijani footballers: the Georgian forward Georgi Adamia, whose signing for Qarabag came about courtesy of a very special advocate.

'When I came to the end of my contract with Inter Baku in the summer of 2010, I was contacted by the Qarabag manager,' Adamia tells me. 'Gurbanov and I had been team-mates at Neftchi and we won the Azerbaijani league together in 2005. Gurban also managed me while I was at Neftchi. If it hadn't been for him, I would never have signed for Qarabag.'

Adamia and Agolli both played in Guzanli and told me what the experience meant for them, with the team going back to its fans, who had since lost their homes and were living in refugee camps. But, above all, they explain why, after two seasons, the club decided to leave Guzanli and return to Baku.

'We would go there to play two days before the game,' explains Agolli. 'We would have a five-hour coach journey from Baku every time. The Qarabag players continued living and training in the capital.

'For almost two hours of the journey, the road surface was poor. The bus would move around a lot. There was accommodation for the players near the stadium and we slept three to a room. What struck me most about Guzanli was that there was hardly anyone in the streets, but whenever we stepped out on to the pitch, the stands were always packed. It's true that the stadium wasn't all that big, but all the seats were occupied and people crowded outside the stadium just for the chance to see the pitch.'

This is echoed by Adamia, 'Unfortunately, there were no trains to the Agdam region. The town of Guzanli was small and quiet, close to the ceasefire line with the Armenian-occupied areas. The people there were very hospitable and kind.'

'Sometimes,' Ansi Agolli remembers, 'we would stay for a whole week, as many as ten days when two consecutive league and cup fixtures were scheduled back-to-back. But usually, two days before a game, we would leave from Baku and go straight back afterwards. Five hours to get there and the same again to get back. We would have to do it at least once every two weeks. It was a very difficult time: we were too tired. We didn't have a pitch to train on or a proper home ground. The situation tested us, not just physically, but also in our heads. It's not easy to put into words what we experienced during my first few years at Qarabag, but I believe that those difficulties did us good and made us stronger. They gave us the chance to carry on building a winning side.'

The warmth of the fans was not enough to build a truly competitive club; Guzanli was too hard to reach from Baku. The village lacked the necessary facilities or infrastructure to host international standard teams.

* * *

Baku, 22 November 2017

'I was in Guzanli back then,' Arthur Huizinga tells me over a cup of tea in a city-centre bar. 'Just a couple of streets and no hotels for visiting fans or opposing teams. That was it. There was just a tiny hotel near the stadium, with no hot water. And just five kilometres away, towards the 94 ceasefire line, there were still snipers.'

Snipers, gunmen.

'Imagine playing a Champions League game there!' Arthur exclaims.

In 2012/13, Qarabag went back to playing their home games in Baku, at the Tofiq Bahramov Stadium, which had been their home for European cup matches over the years. Gurbanov's team finished the league season second in the table, three points behind Neftchi, who secured their eighth domestic title since independence. Glory went to the Brazilian attacking midfielder Richard Almeida, who, in his first season in Azerbaijan after arriving from the Portuguese team Gil Vicente, was top scorer with 13 goals in 30 league games. Almeida was matched by his compatriot Reynaldo, who wasted no time pulling off impressive feats in a black shirt for the Agdam Horsemen, and, not forgetting, as always, the captain Rashad Sadigov, Gara Garayev, Vuqar Nadirov, Maksim Medvedev, Dutchman Leroy George, and the Macedonian playmaker Muarem Muarem, in the number ten shirt.

The Gozal brothers' project, the decision to entrust the team, without so much as a hesitation or backward glance, to Gurban Gurbanov, achieved its objective the following year.

'You want to know what happened during those years?' says Ansi Agolli. 'We worked hard! The team didn't change much and, if it did, it was only to improve our game or put into practice what Gurbanov was asking for and is still asking for.'

The following season, they reached the pinnacle with a resounding 4-1 win at Inter Baku on 7 May 2014, two games from the end of the league season. Qarabag bagged their second title to add to the one achieved the year Agdam fell. In the sixth year of Gurbanov's tenure, the 13th under Azersun ownership, the longed-for victory came 21 years after the final sealed against Khazar Sumgayit with a goal from Yashar Huseynov, two minutes from the end of the regulation 90.

'I never played in Guzanli because Qarabag were already back playing in Baku by the time I arrived,' says Richard Almeida, a member of the 2013/14 champions. 'I don't know the real reason why the club decided to move back to the capital, but I think it was to do with the long journey they had to make for every game. What I do know for sure is that once they decided to go back to Baku, giving us the chance to rest from all the travelling, we were able to become champions. Living and playing in the capital helped us a lot. But we've never forgotten and never will forget the people of Agdam. They give us the strength to fight and leave the pitch with a win. Every time we win, it's as if they're there with us.'

The day after the title was secured, I had the opportunity to interview Qarabag's Muarem Muarem for the Eurasianet.org website, which I was working for at the time.

'This is my first trophy in Azerbaijan,' the Macedonian player told me, 'and I'm delighted. Now we have some great opportunities in the games ahead of us in Europe and I'm convinced we'll give everything we've got to stay in the competition for as long as possible. I've been here for two and a half years now and I can say I really feel at home after some teething problems.'

Then Muarem added, 'We're the only ones who know how tough it was to win this title again after 21 years. I'm happy in Baku because we've got all the comforts we need living here, but we haven't forgotten Agdam. This trophy is for the people who live there.'

The whole team, technical staff and management went straight to the Agdam region, to the refugee camps, to take the trophy they had won back to their people.

That day was to be the start of a winning run – in Azerbaijan and in Europe – that would lead Qarabag to five consecutive domestic titles, the last of which was won on 22 April 2018 with four games to spare, thanks to a 1-0 victory in Sumgait that bore the hallmark of the Spanish player Dani Quintana.

The season that followed the second league title, 2014/15, brought definitive consecration at European level. For the first time in their history, Qarabag found themselves in Champions League qualifying. However, after brilliantly overcoming the Maltese team Valletta, they were knocked out by the Austrians from Salzburg: a 2-1 win at the Tofiq Bahramov, with goals scored by Danilo Dias and Reynaldo, was followed by a 2-0 defeat in Austria that relegated Gurbanov's team to the Europa League play-offs. It was the fourth play-off for Qarabag – after the losses against FC Twente, Borussia Dortmund and Club Brugge – and the draw had served up the Azerbaijani team with a chance for revenge against the Dutch. This time the story would have a very different ending.

A goalless draw in Baku made talk of qualification less convincing and, when the former Inter Milan player

Luc Castaignos put the home team ahead in the 37th minute of the return leg in Enschede, a chill descended on the hopes of the travelling Azerbaijani fans. But, in the 51st minute, Muarem found the goal to make it 1-1, gifting qualification to his team due to the away goals rule. Qarabag would play in the group stage of the Europa League for the first time. The Azerbaijani team was drawn in Group F alongside the Italians of Inter Milan, the Ukrainian team Dnipro and the French side Saint-Étienne.

On 13 November 2014, Konami, a popular Japanese video game development and design company, unveiled the latest edition of its *Pro Evolution Soccer*, as it did every year. For the first time, Qarabag were one of the teams that gamers could pick to play with.

Against all odds, Qarabag narrowly missed out on getting through the groups to qualify for the knockout stage. After a goalless draw at home against Saint-Étienne on their debut and a 2-0 loss to Inter at the San Siro, the team captained by Rashad Sadigov went on to win 1-0 in Ukraine against the experienced Dnipro, thanks once again to a goal by Muarem, who always seemed to score when it mattered. At the end of the first sequence of the group games, Qarabag found themselves in contention for a second-place finish that would guarantee them passage to the next round. A 2-1 home defeat to Dnipro complicated things, but the 1-1 draw in France – with a goal from Vuqar Nadirov – and Inter's simultaneous 2-1 win over the Ukrainians meant that it would come down to the last round of games: Dnipro would take on Saint-Étienne while Qarabag faced Inter. The Italian side were top of the group with 11 points, followed by Saint-Étienne and Qarabag on five, and Dnipro just behind on four. With the Nerazzurri already through, all three of the other teams were still in with a chance of qualification for the next stage.

On 11 December 2014 at the Tofiq Bahramov in Baku, the atmosphere was worthy of a grand occasion, the 31,200 paying spectators were expecting to witness an appointment with history. These were the two teams that took to the pitch under the watchful eye of referee Miroslav Zelinka from the Czech federation:

Qarabag: Šehić, Agolli, Sadigov, Guseynov, Medvedev, Richard Almeida, Qarayev, Muarem, George (Gurbanov 60), Alaskarov, Nadirov (Yusifov 43). Manager: Gurban Gurbanov

Inter Milan: Carrizo, Campagnaro, Donkor, Andreolli, D'Ambrosio (Dimarco 84), M'Vila, Krhin, Obi (Baldini 91), Mbaye, Bonazzoli, Osvaldo. Manager: Roberto Mancini

As Inter's qualification was already mathematically guaranteed, Mancini fielded a side of reserves and young players against a Qarabag team going all out for the win. What resulted was an unpleasant encounter that culminated in something the Italian Eurosport.it journalist Alessandro Dinoia said was 'a pity fate had already decided that the fans from the ghost town would be cheated by the clearest ghost qualification in recent decades of European football'.

In the 94th minute, with the score at 0-0 and Dnipro in the lead against Saint-Étienne, putting the Ukrainians in second place with seven points, the Brazilian Richard Almeida pounced on the ball just inside the box and passed the keeper Carrizo with a daring shot. The TV images clearly show the Inter defenders putting their heads in their hands in disappointment at the conceded goal which, for Qarabag, would have meant victory, second place and historic qualification for the knockout stage of the Europa League. The home supporters started celebrating, as did the players on the pitch, but the referee Zelinka, following the recommendation of his assistant and compatriot Pelikan, disallowed the goal due to an alleged touch from the Dutch player Leroy, in an offside position. No one on the pitch or in the stands was in any doubt that the deflection responsible for wrong-footing Inter's Argentine goalkeeper had come from his team-mate Donkor.

'When I scored that goal,' Richard tells me, 'I knew we'd qualified, as did the whole stadium. Everyone was celebrating and when the referee disallowed the goal, we all felt sad and angry. In that moment I wanted to kill the referee because he'd turned our dream into a nightmare, all the more so because we were beating a team like Inter Milan! But that's football and it's all water under the bridge.'

After three further consecutive eliminations in the third qualifying round of the Champions League, and as many Europa League play-offs and group-stage eliminations, after facing opponents of the calibre of Tottenham, Monaco, Fiorentina, Celtic and Anderlecht, which served only to bolster Qarabag's international experience and, at the same time, spread the word about its story and that of the city of Agdam around the continent, came the summer of 2017.

The draw for the first Champions League qualifying round pitted the Horsemen against the Georgian team Samtredia, who were easily overcome in the first leg with a 5-0 home win. This was followed by another victory at the Boris Paichadze Dinamo Arena in Tbilisi, 1-0 this time thanks to the goal scored by Haitian full-back Wilde-Donald Guerrier, a recent signing from the Turkish side Alanyaspor. Qarabag's opponents in the second qualifying round were much more formidable: the Moldovans of Sheriff Tiraspol, managed by Roberto Bordin. A goalless draw in Baku followed a precious 2-1 win, with goals scored by the Spaniard Míchel and the South African striker Dino Ndlovu, who led Qarabag into the play-offs for a place in the Champions League group stage. This was a historically significant result for the whole of Azerbaijani football, given that only Neftchi had ever gone so far in Europe's top club competition.

Gurbanov's side would face Copenhagen, a team that had played in the Champions League group stage before. In 2010/11, they had even qualified for the second phase behind Barcelona and ahead of Panathinaikos and Rubin Kazan, before eventually falling to Chelsea in the round of 16.

Ansi Agolli remembers, 'After the draw, when we found out we were going to play Copenhagen, we knew we were facing a team with a great European pedigree. A week before the first leg, Gurbanov showed us lots of videos of Copenhagen. He made us watch them all three times! We analysed the team player by player, their strengths and weaknesses. The biggest danger for us was set pieces, free kicks and corners, when the ball came down into the area, given their size. As for us, the manager told us to play our football, like we knew how to play. We had a method and we shouldn't change it. Gurbanov always asked us not to change our style, to always play our football, even if we were facing strong opposition.'

The day of the first leg arrived – at the Tofiq Bahramov in Baku as usual – on 15 August 2017.

'One detail that paid off in that game was that we played with a high defensive line,' explains Agolli. 'The manager told us to stay high, and whenever we picked up the ball in midfield, to break immediately. There's no doubt that this approach paid off, given we scored the goal that decided the game on a counter attack.'

The goal scored by 20-year-old striker Mahir Madatov brought the first 90 minutes to a close with the scoreboard showing 1-0 for Qarabag, a good result ahead of the crucial clash on Danish soil, but not enough to be able to afford distractions.

Ansi said, 'We knew Copenhagen's real strength was at home. We'd studied their two-leg tie against Vardar Skopje, when they beat the Macedonians 4-1 at their home ground after going down 1-0 in the first leg. In the videos we'd seen that their football at home was about "all for one", very aggressive and with real pressure. We prepared ourselves for a battle. It was the match of our lives.'

'How do you prepare for the match of your life?' I ask Ansi.

'You have to leave no stone unturned. There was a serious atmosphere throughout the team. Everyone was doing their job and they knew the time had come to show their strength and our team spirit. The moment had come to bring all the sacrifices we'd made and the work we'd done on to the pitch. Our time had come.'

On 23 August 2017, Qarabag took to the field at Copenhagen's Telia Parken Stadium in the full knowledge that they had an appointment with history. Here are the players picked to line up for the battle, as Ansi Agolli described it:

Copenhagen: R. Olsen, Ankersen, Luftner, Boilesen, Bengtsson, Verbič, Gregus, Kvist, Kusk, Pavlović, Santander. Manager: Stale Solbakken

Qarabag (4-3-3): Šehić, Medvedev, Rzeźniczak, Huseynov, Agolli, Richard Almeida, Míchel, Garayev, Madatov, Ndlovu, Guerrier. Manager: Gurban Gurbanov

The hosts went ahead as the Spanish referee Alberto Undiano Mallenco had the whistle in his mouth ready to signal the end of the first half; the Paraguayan Federico Santander took advantage when the Qarabag keeper Šehić came off his line, heading it up over him to give the Danish team the lead and silence any premature talk of qualification.

In the 62nd minute, the outcome of the tie would take a definitive turn. After sprinting down the left wing, Ansi Agolli crossed the ball into the box, where Dino Ndlovu was quick to pick it up before firing it past the incredulous Danish keeper, Olsen, at the far post. Not even Pavlović's goal four minutes later could challenge the historic result: Qarabag Agdam were the first Azerbaijani team in history to reach the group stage of the Champions League.

A peak that was high, very high, incredible and unthinkable only a few years earlier for a team that hasn't played at home since 23 July 1993.

'It was the best page we'd ever written in our history,' explains Emrah Celikel. 'I'm convinced that any goal is achievable if you believe in it, with experience and by staying close like a family.'

Journalist Shakir Eminbeyli goes somewhat against the opinion that those kinds of results were unthinkable for the team from Agdam, 'In my view, we, as fans of the team, expected the successes that Qarabag have achieved in recent years. We always hoped and trusted in the club. Because in modern sport in general, and in football in particular, many, if not all ,aspects are resolved by a club's financial position. But desire, ambition and belief in your own strengths sometimes exceed the hierarchies dictated by money.

'History is full of these kinds of examples. Our club's budget is infinitely lower than those of the teams that usually take part in the Champions and Europa League group games. And from a technical point of view, our players are of a lower standard than our European rivals. But, as we've seen, the fighting and determined spirit of our boys has once again demonstrated that this factor has an important role to play in achieving any objective.'

After six games in the Champions League group stage, Qarabag had achieved international consecration and not disgraced themselves, thanks above all to two draws against Atlético Madrid and a narrow loss to Roma. But the question I asked myself and the people I spoke to when writing this book was this: 25 years on, does it still make sense to refer to Qarabag as a team from Agdam? What place does Agdam, the ghost city, the Hiroshima of the Caucasus, now hold in the victories and life of a team that has increasingly taken on the dimension of a side from the Azerbaijani capital?

12

Qarabag and the legacy of Agdam

'I'M NOT from Agdam,' says Shakir Eminbeyli, 'but I've been there a million times, before and after the war with Armenia. I had lots of friends there. I was young and was one of the first TV war reporters at the time of independence. I visited the whole Karabakh region and the other villages that were the scenes of clashes on the border with Armenia.

'I saw Agdam's beautiful gardens and the city's jovial, hard-working, self-sufficient and affluent people. I saw the most beautiful horses, squares, streets, schools, the cultural building, museums and the picturesque Eastern market in that wonderful city. I admired its simple architecture, the mosque with its stunning minarets. I quenched my thirst with delicious tea, sipped in the unique Tea House. Finally, I watched a Qarabag game in Agdam!

'Unfortunately, I was also an eyewitness to the city's occupation. I filmed the horrors of war and death, the death of innocent children and elderly people in that peaceful city. It was tragic and sickening to witness the destruction and fall of the city. Painful. But remembering all that makes me feel even worse.'

'What do you think is left of Agdam today?' I ask him.

'I'm an adult now. The person who witnessed all those horrors was just a boy. That city is no longer there. It's just ruins, a ghost town. But personally, I think it's worse for the Armenians. Now they have to go to the city they devastated, a soulless and lifeless place. If the Armenian soldiers have any humanity, they must be suffering and feeling even more disgusted than we are. Because they're guilty of what's happened to what was once a wonderful city.'

'Would you agree if I said that the Qarabag team is all that remains of Agdam? Or that Agdam is still alive as long as the team continues to exist to remind the whole world of its story?'

Shakir replies, 'Qarabag FK is not just a team for those who lived in Agdam, but for the whole nation. The Azerbaijani people have all suffered the pain of the occupation of the Karabakh region. After the sorrow felt over Karabakh, our people cannot help but support Qarabag, which has the same name as the area. Whenever we say Qarabag, we mean Azerbaijan.'

Shakir then gives himself away with a prediction, 'I'm sure once our land has been liberated from occupation, Qarabag FK will go from strength to strength. I don't think any team would be able to take a single point off them at the Imaret.'

'How long will it be until then, do you think?'

'In a couple of years Agdam will return to our homeland. I'm confident it can happen.'

Qarabag's presence in the Champions League was like a megaphone, letting the whole continent know about the reality of a team that hasn't played at home since 1993, whose fans are mostly refugees, displaced by war.

'When they qualified for the group stage in Copenhagen,' Ambassador Augusto Massari told me in Baku, 'lots of media outlets and fans from all over Europe wondered what Qarabag was. The Azerbaijanis did well at using the team as a tool to attract international attention and to merge it with a problem that was fundamentally important to them.'

I also addressed these issues with Mammad Ahmadzada, the ambassador of the Republic of Azerbaijan in Rome. Together we discussed future prospects for the nation as a whole, which is now increasingly focused on assuming a role of greater importance within Europe. Sport is becoming an image vehicle, a constant advertisement for the potential of a country with one foot in the east but increasingly looking west, an ideal bridge between two such different, but similar, worlds.

'Not just football, but sport in general has taken on huge significance for Azerbaijan in recent years,' said Ahmadzada. 'This has multiple value. First of all, my country is focused on investing in the younger generation. Baku is an official candidate to host Expo 2025 and the slogan behind our candidacy is "Developing Human Capital, Building a Better Future". The sporting world is closely linked to young people and this is one of the reasons we invest in it greatly. Furthermore, the

Azerbaijani economy has been on a path of differentiation for years, and sport favours this trend. Added to this, we've proven ourselves as organisers of international sporting events.

'Just think of the Baku 2015 European Games, which also guaranteed the country state-of-the-art facilities to be used afterwards for top-level competitions. We hosted the Islamic Solidarity Games in 2017 and have been an important stage on the Formula 1 GP tour for two years. As well as the next Grand Prix stages, the UEFA Europa League Final will be held at the Baku Olympic Stadium in 2019, plus four games during the 2020 Euros. All this also promotes awareness of Azerbaijan as a tourist destination. Football is part of this context because it's the most popular sport in the country and has a place in all our hearts. It makes me very happy to see Azerbaijan begin to reap some success on the football pitch and Qarabag's results are clear evidence of this.'

'Qarabag Agdam have achieved a prestigious milestone this year with participation in the Champions League group stage. What does this football team represent for your country and what significance do their achievements have?' I ask.

'For Azerbaijanis, Qarabag is their most loved team, beyond individual footballing affiliations. For us they're a team that symbolises the struggle we continue to fight every day to free our territories occupied by Armenia. The success of Qarabag has a dual impact: on the one hand sporting, on the other human, because it allows us to remind the world of the dramatic story of the team and our country.'

'Mr Ambassador, do you really believe that Qarabag will play in Agdam again one day?'

'Absolutely, yes. We always repeat this, but they're not just words: Azerbaijan will never reconcile with the military occupation of its territories. I'm sure we'll succeed in getting back what belongs to us. We will use every means possible to restore our sovereignty and territorial integrity. The refugees will all be able to return to their homes and Qarabag will be able to go back to Agdam. I continue to hope, like all my people, that this can happen through diplomatic channels, but in order for it to happen, the intervention of the international community is also required.

'Through the experiences in Jojug Merjanly and Shikharkh, the Azerbaijani state has shown once again that we will never accept the occupation of our territories. Both villages were once under occupation, but were freed from the Armenian invaders and are now beautiful places, where thousands of families have been transferred to new homes and been able to start new lives,' he replies, referring to the territories liberated following the so-called Four-Day War in April 2016.

By comparison, here are the thoughts of Emrah Celikel on the existence of Agdam and its links to the football team and its success: 'Everyone knows that Agdam is part of Karabakh and Azerbaijan. We're aware of how sensitive Karabakh's position is for Azerbaijan. We understand the responsibility we're honoured to have for the entire nation. We play and represent every refugee from Azerbaijan and the city of Agdam, the heart of Karabakh. The whole region supports us and cheers for us when we win. Our success, such as reaching the Champions League, always raises the hope of the people of Agdam and the whole of Azerbaijan that one day we'll be able to play back at the Imaret again.'

* * *

21 November 2017
Baku Olympic Stadium

'I think everyone in the team knows how important this game is. We respect Chelsea and I think the first leg didn't really reflect what Qarabag is. It didn't represent the team or the people of Agdam.'

This was the opinion of Dino Ndlovu, South African centre-forward for Qarabag Agdam FK, an opinion shared at the start of the official press conference held the day before the Champions League game against Chelsea. Dino signed for the Azerbaijani club in the summer of 2016. He has not seen Agdam, never played at the Imaret, nor has he ever been to Nagorno-Karabakh. And yet he chose to mention the name of the city, the city that no longer exists, on the eve of the greatest achievement in Qarabag's history: a home game against the champions of England, Antonio Conte's Chelsea. I was struck by the fact that Dino's first thought when asked about the game was for Agdam and its people. What Ndlovu said contained the true secret of Qarabag, the real answer to my question.

'We'll do our best,' explains Celikel, 'to keep the name Qarabag Agdam for our club and to ensure that all our players are aware of what the team they play for really represents. We give them all the information they need and explain why Qarabag is currently based in Baku instead of Agdam. This provides them with real motivation. We don't play like a football team: we play like the Qarabag family and we represent Agdam. This is the secret behind our success.'

A family, that's what Qarabag is. A family in which Shahid Hasanov, aged 61, is responsible for the club's licences and prepares the paperwork before every game.

'Thank God for technology!' he exclaims when I ask him if it's true that he still fills out all the documents by hand. 'I only use a pen for the team sheets, the lists of players that go to the referee.'

It is a family in which Mushfiq Huseynov is Gurbanov's deputy, in which Elshad Khudadatov trains the youth team. Many people who experienced the years before the occupation, who played at the Imaret, are still at the club. Their key role is to pass down the name of Agdam and the story of a team that is more than a football team to present and future generations. A family.

13

IDP

Internal displacement in Azerbaijan is mainly a consequence of the ethnic conflict over the territory of Nagorno-Karabakh. The roots of the conflict go back to early Soviet times, when Nagorno-Karabakh was declared an autonomous region within Azerbaijan. Ethnic conflict erupted in 1988 when the Soviet government of Armenia agreed with Nagorno-Karabakh to incorporate it into Armenia. Nagorno-Karabakh declared its own independence in 1992, leading to war between Karabakh Armenian and Azerbaijani forces. Active hostilities ended with a ceasefire agreement in 1994, but Nagorno-Karabakh's independence claim has not been recognised by Azerbaijan, Armenia or any other state, and a final resolution to the conflict is still pending. Nagorno-Karabakh and seven surrounding districts have been wholly or partially occupied by ethnic Armenian forces ever since. The State

Committee for Refugees and IDPs is the sole source of statistics on internal displacement. In early 2010, the committee put the number of IDPs at 586,013 (Government of Azerbaijan, 1 January 2010). The vast majority are ethnic Azeri, though there are also ethnic Kurdish, Russian and Turkish IDPs (CoE, 24 May 2007; UN Commission for Human Rights 25 January 1999, para. 31).

Prior to the conflict, ethnic Azeris were a minority in Nagorno-Karabakh but made up the overwhelming majority of the population of 425,000 in seven adjacent districts. More than 400,000 were displaced from these areas during the conflict (Refugee Survey Quarterly, 2009).

This document is taken from the website of the IDMC, the International Displacement Monitoring Centre, a non-governmental organisation that has been monitoring and compiling statistics and reports on the condition of those defined as internally displaced persons around the world since 1988.

The UNHRC, the United Nations High Commission on Refugees, says the following:

'At the end of 2019, some 45.7 million people were internally displaced due to armed conflict, generalised violence or human rights violations, according to the Internal Displacement Monitoring Centre (IDMC).

'Internally displaced persons (IDPs), according to the United Nations Guiding Principles on Internal

Displacement, are "persons or groups of persons who have been forced or obliged to flee or to leave their homes or places of habitual residence, in particular as a result of or in order to avoid the effects of armed conflict, situations of generalised violence, violations of human rights or natural or human-made disasters, and who have not crossed an internationally recognised state border".

'This, however, is a descriptive definition, which does not confer a special legal status because IDPs, being inside their country, remain entitled to all the rights and guarantees as citizens and other habitual residents of their country. As such, national authorities have the primary responsibility to prevent forced displacement and to protect IDPs.'

Global figures fell slightly last year, but the numbers remain staggering: the annual IDMC report estimated that, as of October 2017, around 40.3 million people were internally displaced due to armed conflict, generalised violence or human rights violations. And the Nagorno-Karabakh conflict has given Azerbaijan the unenviable record of the highest number of IDPs per capita.

Qarabag Agdam exists to represent those million people who have lost their homes, families and roots, to carry their voices across Europe and shove their uncomfortable presence in the face of public opinion. Their existence disturbs the consciences of a continent that has been dealing with a conflict for 30 years that none of the powers involved wants to end, for their own gain.

As stated in 1998 by Bill Clinton during his presidency of the USA, 'The actions taken by the government of

Armenia in the context of the conflict over Nagorno-Karabakh are inconsistent with the territorial integrity and national sovereignty principles of the Helsinki Final Act. Armenia supports Nagorno-Karabakh separatists in Azerbaijan both militarily and financially. Nagorno-Karabakh forces, assisted by units of the Armenian armed forces, currently occupy the Nagorno-Karabakh region and surrounding areas in Azerbaijan. This violation and the restoration of peace between Armenia and Azerbaijan have been taken up by the OSCE.'

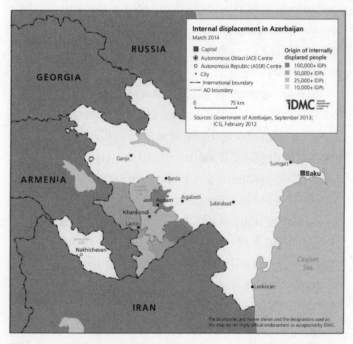

The map of IDPs in Azerbaijan prepared by the IDMC, updated in September 2013 (source: Government of the Republic of Azerbaijan)

The number of people registered as IDPs by the Refugee Committee of the Government of Azerbaijan as a result of the Nagorno-Karabakh conflict was estimated at 622,892 in December 2014. As the same state body quantifies those who have returned to their home areas at 54,000, the IDMC estimates that the real number of IDPs in Azerbaijan is currently around 569,000. Most of these have been unable to return due to the lack of a peace agreement.

These 569,000 IDPs are estimated to include 230,000 children born to internally displaced persons during exile.

The vast majority of IDPs who migrated during the war, between 1988 and 1994, are of Azerbaijani ethnicity, but the total also includes around 4,000 Kurds, present in the regions of Lachin and Kalbajar, plus others of Russian and Turkish ethnicity.

Far more than from Nagorno-Karabakh itself, the majority of internally displaced people come from the seven occupied territories that surround it. In particular, of the 569,000 IDPs from the Armenian-occupied western parts of Azerbaijan, according to data from the United States Committee for Refugees (USCR), about 42,000 come from Nagorno-Karabakh. The others include refugees from neighbouring regions: Fizuli (133,725), Agdam (128,584), Lachin (63,007), Kalbajar (59,724), Gubadli (31,276), Zangilan (34,797), Terter (5,171) and Adjabedi (3,358).

Internally displaced people are present in all 69 districts of Azerbaijan, but about half live in the capital Baku. About 32 per cent live in public places made available by the government as temporary accommodation at the beginning of the transfer. The accommodation found for these displaced people includes abandoned railway carriages in old disused yards. A quarter live in new homes built by the government for the purpose, 20 per cent with relatives and 12 per cent in makeshift accommodation. Finally, a number of IDPs equal to about eight per cent of the total occupy property owned by others.

Finally, there is one further fact I would like to highlight. The last census carried out in the Soviet Union before its demise dates from 1989: in that year there were 192,000 people residing in Karabaka, of whom 76 per cent were Armenians, 23 per cent Azeris and the remainder Russians, Kurds, Greeks and Assyrians.

By 2008, however, the new census conducted by the authorities of the self-proclaimed Nagorno-Karabakh Republic, or Artsakh, calculated a population in Karabakh equal to 139,900 inhabitants, which breaks down into 95 per cent Armenians and 5 per cent Assyrians, Greeks and Kurds. The Azeris have all been forced to leave the region.

14

The Champions League

ON 12 September 2017, Qarabag's Champions League adventure began at London's Stamford Bridge against Chelsea, Antonio Conte's champions of England. These were the starting 11s:

Chelsea: Courtois, Azpilicueta, Christensen, Cahill, Zappacosta, Kanté, Fàbregas, Marcos Alonso, Willian, Pedro, Batshuayi. Manager: Antonio Conte

Qarabag: Šehić, Medvedev, Huseynov, R. Sadigov, Rzeźniczak, Garayev, Pedro Henrique, Míchel, Richard Almeida, Guerrier, Ndlovu. Manager: Gurban Gurbanov

Qarabag paid for the inexperience and excitement of their debut and were outclassed 6-0 thanks to goals from Pedro, Zappacosta, Azpilicueta, Bakayoko, Batshuayi and an own goal from Medvedev, eight minutes from the final whistle. Zappacosta's goal in particular was extraordinary, with the Italian right-back managing to outwit Šehić from a distance after a long, solo run from his own back line.

The second matchday in Group C marked Qarabag's home debut in the opening stage of Europe's top competition, against Eusebio di Francesco's Roma at the Olympic Stadium in Baku. There had been a great deal of discussion about the team from Agdam playing their Champions League home games at the capital's new stadium instead of the Tofiq Bahramov, which had become their customary European venue during the Gurbanov era. The decision was made based on the capacity of the new stadium – 68,700 seats compared to the 31,200-seater Tofiq Bahramov. There were concerns in the local press that Qarabag had played too few games in the modern stadium built for the first European Games, held in Baku in 2015.

'We've definitely moved around a lot over the years. We've played almost everywhere, especially in the stadiums around Baku,' remembers Ansi Agolli. 'But there's no doubt that the stadium that most feels like home is the Tofiq Bahramov. It's where we've spent most of our life as a team and where we've had our greatest achievements. Personally, I wouldn't have chosen to play the Champions League at the Olympic, but I understand that the demand for tickets prompted the club and the federation to make that choice. But we've definitely experienced our best moments and highest highs at what used to be the Republic Stadium.'

On 27 September 2017, *Corriere della Sera* reported: 'Qarabag hope the home factor in Baku will help bridge the technical gap between them and the Giallorossi. "We definitely have to do better in defence," explains Dani Quintana. "We have to make sure we don't make mistakes and capitalise on the chances we'll get. We're stronger in Baku and Roma won't find it easy to come here and play.'"

In an exclusive interview granted to me and published on the *Corriere della Sera* website, the Spaniard Dani Quintana – at Qarabag Agdam since 2015 – was clearly looking forward to the game against AS Roma at Baku's Olympic Stadium.

That same day, in front of 67,200 cheering spectators, Qarabag scored their first goal after conceding two to Manolas and Džeko inside the first 15 minutes. By now, the adjective 'historic' was becoming redundant. Qarabag's goal was scored by the Brazilian Pedro Henrique – an attacking winger on loan from the Greek team PAOK Thessaloniki – who capitalised on a mistake by the Frenchman Gonalons. Qarabag twice came close to equalising in the dying moments of the game, proving that they would not be the sacrificial victims of the group as everyone had assumed.

Here are the two team line-ups:

Qarabag: Šehić, Medvedev, Huseynov, Sadigov, Agolli, Richard, Garayev, Pedro Henrique (Elyounoussi 76), Míchel, Madatov, Ndlovu. Manager: Gurbanov

Roma: Alisson, Peres, Manolas, Jesus, Kolarov, Pellegrini (Strootman 81), Gonalons (De Rossi 67), Nainggolan, Defrel (Florenzi 57), Džeko, El Shaarawy. Manager: Di Francesco

In the third round of matches in the group, the team captained by Rashad Sadigov hosted Diego Simeone's Atlético Madrid at home. Twice Champions League finalists in the previous five years, they were desperate for points to keep them within touching distance of Roma. The Italians were in second behind Chelsea and already on four points after the first two games, compared with just one point for the Spanish team, after to a goalless draw against Roma. But a trap had been set for the Spaniards at the Olympic Stadium: Qarabag secured their first point, holding Atlético to a goalless draw. It was an excellent defensive performance from the team from Agdam, who went down to ten men in the last 15 minutes due to a second yellow card shown to Dino Ndlovu. Despite this, they came within a whisker of a sensational goal thanks to the Norwegian Elyounoussi, who nearly gifted Qarabag the win in the 90th minute on the break.

Qarabag: Šehić, Medvedev (Rzeźniczak 71), Guseynov, Sadigov, Agolli, Pedro Henrique (Guerrier 69), Richard, Míchel (Elyounoussi 85), Garayev, Madatov, Ndlovu. Manager: Gurbanov

Atlético Madrid: Oblak, Vrsaljko, Godín, Giménez, Filipe Luís, Gaitan (Partey 64), Saul, Gabi, Carrasco (Correa 72), Griezmann, Gameiro (Torres 72). Manager: Simeone

Two weeks later, the Horsemen in black pulled off an even more unbelievable feat against the backdrop of the new Wanda Metropolitano Stadium in Madrid, Diego Simeone's team's new home since 16 September. When Gurbanov's side stepped out on to the pitch against the Colchoneros on the evening of 30 October, everyone was predicting an Atlético win. This was the game that was expected to secure the Spanish's team's first three points of their, so far, disappointing Champions League campaign. Qarabag were seen by fans of the Madrid team and the media as the opponents against whom the ambitious Atlético simply had to get a win.

But, after an important save from Šehić following a dangerous strike by Gameiro and a recurring theme of a match that would see Atlético keep possession of the ball and Qarabag break on the counter, something no one expected happened in the 40th minute. The Haitian Guerrier took a left-footed corner kick from the right-hand side and found the head of Míchel, in the middle of the box. The Spanish midfielder, formerly with Getafe, Birmingham City and AEK Athens, then found the back of Oblak's net. Qarabag Agdam sent shockwaves around the Wanda Metropolitano as they took a 1-0 lead.

Šehić defended the Azerbaijani goal from Spanish attack on several occasions as the Madrid team pushed hard for an equaliser, holding out until the 56th minute, when the Ghanaian Thomas Partey fired a long-range shot into the top-left corner. The game ended 1-1 and Qarabag had won the second Champions League point in their history. Atlético Madrid, on the other hand, were still languishing in third place, a position that, only two games from the end of the group stage, was an ongoing cause for concern for Simeone's team. The Bosnian goalkeeper Ibrahim Šehić, who joined Qarabag in 2013, was the hero of the night. Stefano Fonsato of Eurosport, who named him man of the match and rated his performance an eight out of ten, said the following, 'Ibrahim Šehić (Qarabag) – superlative performance. A portcullis in the face of the, albeit not irresistible, Atlético Madrid attack.'

Atlético Madrid: Oblak, Juanfran, Savić, Godín, Filipe Luís, Saul Ñíguez, Gabi, Partey (Gaitan 62), Correa, Griezmann, Gameiro (Fernando Torres 70). Manager: Simeone

Qarabag: Šehić, Garayev, Agolli, Medvedev, Rzeźniczak, Sadigov, Pedro Henrique, Richard Almeida, Guerrier (Yunuszade 63), Míchel (Ismaiylov 90+2), Sheydaev (Dani Quintana 72). Manager: Gurbanov

The day after the draw at the Wanda Metropolitano brought another result that would go down in the annals of the Azerbaijani team. Qarabag played their fourth Group C game in the UEFA Youth League – the parallel Champions League for the youth teams of clubs playing in the main competition – at the Estadio Cerro del Espino in Majadahonda. The Horsemen scored a 1-0 win against their Atlético Madrid counterparts thanks to a goal from Yaroslav Deda, a Ukrainian striker born in 1999. The Qarabag team taking part in the Youth League was coached by Rashad Sadigov, the first-team captain, who divided his time between playing on the pitch with the grown-ups and sitting on the bench for the kids. Rashad's fate was already sealed.

Two games from the end, the Champions League Group C table showed Roma on eight points, Chelsea with seven, Atlético Madrid with three and Qarabag on two. On the eve of the game against Chelsea in Baku, Qarabag were still mathematically in the running to qualify for the last 16 or, more realistically, to secure a third-place finish that would grant them passage to the last 32 of the Europa League.

* * *

22 November 2017

'An incredible atmosphere, an icy wind that gets into your bones and a fully militarised zone around the stadium: strict checks on the way in and around 450 soldiers inside, positioned in the stands among the fans and on the sidelines. These are not just fans, but an entire nation.'

These were just some of the notes I took on my way into the press box on a night that would forever mark the history of Qarabag. A team in exile, who had not played at home in front of their fans for almost 25 years, had taken on a new dimension. The whole of Azerbaijan was now their home; the entire population cheered for the team from Agdam and supported their journey around Europe. The stand opposite the press box was united in a mass choreographed display featuring the three colours of the Azerbaijan flag: blue, red and green.

The top row read 'Qarabag'; the second 'The Glorious Qarabag'. The letters that make up the club's name were written on seven separate sheets. It was a proud rather than controversial response to those who had made fun of the Azerbaijani club's supporters when, at the match against Roma, their choreography had been delivered by just seven boys each holding up an A4-size piece of paper bearing the letters Q-A-R-A-B-A-G. In reality, this wasn't the result of a lack of organisation or familiarity with staging high-level displays, but simply a tradition taken from Turkish football – often used as a model and followed closely by fans in Azerbaijan – in which this is customary.

A red banner in the centre read, 'Far away from home but where you belong' with the crescent moon and star. Underneath, in the green row, appeared the word Azərbaycan, expressing a very clear message. It was a recognition given by the city to a team that was not a national side, but a symbol of redemption for a people still at war, who still felt deprived of a portion of their territory, for displaced people and refugees forced to flee their homes reduced to rubble.

Nor was the Imaret forgotten. The glorious stadium – the tomb of the khans, razed to the ground during the war – was reborn under a banner that appeared in the stands at every Qarabag game, with two words in lowercase, written in white on a blue background: Imaret Tayfa.

Zaur Mammadov Zakiroglu was one of the boys holding that banner. 'I was born in the village of Kyasly in the Agdam region,' he tells me. 'The Imaret Fan Club was founded in 2009 by myself and Shukur Javadov, also from Agdam.

'Our first game was on 23 July 2009 in Baku against Rosenborg, the anniversary of the fall of the city, but the fan club was officially founded on 19 November. We're now known as Imaret Tayfa, based in Baku, with Imaret groups in Turkey, Ukraine and Europe.'

Isko Babazade is another of the group's members, 'To us, not just Agdam, but the whole Karabakh region represents the land we're ready to fight for. We're willing to die for our homeland on the battlefield. What remains of Karabakh in the Qarabag FK team is the mindset to keep fighting until the very end. We're the same. We're the generation that was born during the war. We grew up listening to stories about the war.'

Qarabag's new dimension is represented in a tangible way. 'I'm studying in Tbilisi now,' explains Zaur. 'Our members don't just come from Agdam and its region. Qarabag aren't just the team from Agdam anymore. Our members see Qarabag as representing the whole of Azerbaijan. You could say that Qarabag is the real Azerbaijani national side.'

The idea that the founder of the Imaret Fan Club had was taken literally by those at the top of the federation. A few days before the game between Qarabag and Chelsea, on 3 November 2017, Gurban Gurbanov was officially appointed the new manager of the Azerbaijan national team. As his deputy and coach of the under-21 national team, he chose Rashad Sadigov, despite him still being active as a player.

After years of big-name foreign managers, such as Berti Vogts and Robert Prosinečki, Azerbaijani football had chosen to focus on its own elite and finally settled on a way forward. Not least, because there was an important opportunity at stake that the Azerbaijani national side had to try, at all costs, to grasp with both hands. The 2020 European Championship would be played across the continent and Baku was to be one of the 12 venues chosen to host the tournament's matches, including one of the quarter-finals. With the reform of the qualifying structure and the birth of the so-called Nations League, Azerbaijan had the opportunity to qualify for a European

Championship for the first time, with the chance to play on home soil.

If the rumours were to be believed, the choice of Gurbanov was said to have come down from the top, the very top. President Ilham Aliyev is thought to have wanted a manager who was not a federation yes-man like his predecessors, but most importantly someone who could bring their own ideas, choices and charisma to the role.

I think they hoped Gurbanov would become a sort of Valeriy Lobanovskyi, who picked ten of his Dynamo Kyiv side into the USSR team, transferring an understanding of football and a club mindset to the national and international stage.

These were the teams that played in front of the whole of Azerbaijan, there in spirit if not all in body, at the Olympic Stadium in Baku on the evening of 22 November 2017:

Qarabag: Šehić, Medvedev, Sadigov, Rzeźniczak, Agolli, Guerrier, Almeida, Garayev, Madatov, Míchel, Ndlovu. Manager: Gurban Gurbanov

Chelsea: Courtois, Azpilicueta, David Luiz, Rudiger, Zappacosta, Kanté, Fàbregas, Alonso, Willian, Hazard, Pedro. Manager: Antonio Conte

The hosts did not seem overawed at the kick-off. They focused on keeping possession in a way that was becoming their trademark, even against opponents of the highest level, such as Chelsea. After a quarter of an hour, Qarabag came close to a sensational goal to take the lead, with

Míchel rattling the crossbar of Belgian keeper Courtois's goal. But in the 19th minute the game took a direction it became practically impossible to change. The Portuguese referee Manuel De Sousa awarded a penalty to Chelsea for a questionable holding offence apparently committed by Rashad Sadigov on the Brazilian Willian. It did not end there. The referee also brandished a red card at the Qarabag captain. A penalty and a sending-off. Far too severe and excessive a punishment, not to mention unjustified for a team that wanted the chance to play on an equal footing. They would have liked to have been able to show the whole of Europe that they knew how to play, but De Sousa's decision denied the team from Agdam that chance.

Chelsea didn't need the decision given their technical superiority. Qarabag were floored by the referee and, after Hazard made it 1-0 from the penalty spot, were forced to reorganise. They had to come up with a new plan for the game practically from scratch after their original tactics, on which Gurbanov had worked meticulously, had been cast aside by De Sousa's extreme decision. The game was now all but over and Chelsea took home an easy 4-0 win.

The bitterness felt by the Qarabag supporters was tangible, typified by what Asif Askerov told myself and Arthur Huizinga when our eyes met in the mixed zone on the way out of the stadium, 'It happens with all the small teams; they just want to screw us over.'

Words spoken in disappointment, in the disappointment of being unable to fight against one of the giants of European football on equal terms. Qarabag would probably have lost the game anyway, but they would have done so safe in the knowledge that they had tried their hardest to avoid the loss and given their best to achieve a positive result. That they should have been prevented from this burned more than defeat itself.

Even in the last group game – against Roma in Italy – Qarabag, considered the minnows of the group and the whole competition by the media, proved they had the credentials to play in the Champions League and that their qualification had not been a mere fluke. Roma had to win to top the group, while, after Atlético Madrid's victory over the Giallorossi in the penultimate game, Qarabag could no longer aspire to anything other than honouring the competition and surprising Europe yet again.

My report for *La Gazzetta dello Sport* on 4 December 2017 read: 'Penalty and sending-off. The red card received in the game against Chelsea may deprive Rashad Sadigov, the historic Qarabag captain (and coach of the under-19 team that will take on Roma in the Youth League), of the opportunity to play in front of his fans in Europe for one last time. Born in 1982, this could be Sadigov's last season as a footballer. In the game against Roma, the armband will be worn by 28-year-old Maksim Medvedev, a product of the Qarabag Academy, who has spent his whole career at the club. Medvedev is also destined to take over the role of captain from Sadigov in the Azerbaijan national side that is about to embark on a new adventure.

'Robert Prosinečki's designated successor on the Azerbaijan bench is none other than Gurbanov, the Qarabag manager who, in agreement with the club and the federation, will hold both posts. Qarabag, fresh from an impressive 1-0 win against Neftchi and stubbornly topping the table after five consecutive wins, are increasingly becoming a superpower of Azerbaijani football, thanks, in part, to the huge prizes they succeed in securing through their performances on the European stage. As such, the domestic league is in danger of becoming a league with no real opponents for Gurbanov's side.'

The Italian team could only manage a 1-0 win after a header from Diego Perotti in the 53rd minute, and Qarabag waved goodbye to the Champions League with their heads held high. Their only regret was that they had been unable to fully demonstrate their worth in the game against Chelsea in Baku after the whole dimension of the match was changed by a crazed two-fold refereeing decision.

Roma: Alisson, Florenzi, Manolas, Fazio, Kolarov, Nainggolan, De Rossi, Strootman, El Shaarawy (Gerson 72), Džeko, Perotti (Pellegrini 80). Manager: Di Francesco

Qarabag: Šehić, Medvedev, Yunuszade, Rzeźniczak, Guerrier, Garayev, Ismayilov (Quintana 76) Míchel, Almeida, Madatov (Ramazanov 85), Ndlovu (Sheydaev 85). Manager: Gurbanov

Qarabag's next date with Europe's biggest competition would come in the summer of 2018, thanks to their fifth consecutive Azerbaijan title.

'Our first thought after that win was for our fans, for the people and families of Agdam. We hoped that our success would help alleviate the suffering caused by the difficult situation in which they find themselves,' Ansi Agolli told me the day after the club secured their position at the top of the league table with four games to spare.

15

SOCAR

THE YEARS that immediately followed independence were tough for Azerbaijan. The economic figures for the brand-new nation from 1992 to 1994 tell a pitiless story: industrial production was down 38 per cent on 1990 and inflation had reached a record high of 1,234 per cent.

President Heydar Aliyev was so far-sighted that he saw the energy sector as the key to helping the nation overcome the difficult transition period that would guarantee its future development, bringing with it genuine independence. The risk for the fledgeling former USSR countries was remaining dependent on Moscow or the dictates of the multinationals that would come to exploit their resources and raw materials, subordinating them in a way that would have made independence a purely formal status.

Aliyev took control of the negotiations and presided over the signing, on 20 September 1994, of the first ACG (Azeri, Chirag, Gunashli) contract – named after an area of the Caspian Sea that stretches for 432.4

square kilometres and includes the oilfields of Azeri, Chirag and the especially deep sub-marine Gunashli field. The agreement, which has gone down in history as the 'contract of the century', shaped the ambitious prospects of Baku oil; it involved the sale by Azerbaijan of 25 years of exploration and exploitation rights over the ACG oilfields to an international consortium of 11 multinational companies, headed by BP.

The ACG contract was a tool personally devised by the president. It was aimed at guaranteeing Azerbaijan genuine sovereignty and territorial integrity through the creation of a consortium that would bring together the economic and strategic interests of the region's most important players.

Since its signing, investments have been made for the development of the ACG fields equal to approximately $33bn. The first barrel of oil from the field was produced on 7 November 1997.

Based on figures up to 2017, the Caspian Sea area has supplied approximately 3.2 billion barrels, equal to 440 million tonnes of oil, exported to the main global markets. The principal distribution routes of oil from Azerbaijan are the Baku-Tbilisi-Ceyhan pipeline, 1,768km long, which links the Caspian Sea to the Mediterranean; the Baku-Supsa, which reaches the Black Sea, in Georgia, through 833km of piping; and the Baku-Novorossiysk, which, after a journey of 1,330km, emerges in Russia, also in the Black Sea. But the ACG oilfields are not limited to the production of oil. The extraction basin has, in fact, produced a total of over 30 billion cubic metres of gas for the Azerbaijan government. Production from the

ACG fields has now exceeded 585,000 barrels of black gold per day.

SOCAR, the State Oil Company of the Azerbaijan Republic, one of the protagonists in the 1994 agreement and still the leading player at the oilfield, was established by presidential decree number 200 on 13 September 1992. With time, it has become a colossus in the industry. A company worth $20bn dollars, it controls the entire economy of the Caucasian republic, despite the troubled times that followed the collapse of the price of crude oil by more than 40 per cent between 2014 and 2016, even prompting Azerbaijan to ask for help from the International Monetary Fund.

On 14 September 2017, the amended and revised agreement on the joint development and shared production of the Azeri and Chirag fields and the deep-water portion of the Gunashli field was signed by the president of Azerbaijan, Ilham Aliyev, at the Heydar Aliyev Centre in Baku. The new ownership percentages for the ACG contract, following the review, would be as follows: BP, 30.37 per cent; AzAcg (SOCAR), 25 per cent; Chevron, 9.57 per cent; INPEX, 9.31 per cent; Statoil, 7.27 per cent; ExxonMobil, 6.79 per cent; TP, 5.73 per cent, ITOCHU, 3.65 per cent; and ONGC Videsh Limited (OVL), 2.31 per cent. SOCAR's share rose by 11.6 per cent to 25 per cent from 1994 and Azerbaijan's oil profit share would now be 75 per cent, a significant increase on the previous contract.

I have already explained how the history of football in Azerbaijan is closely linked to that of the oil industry, but the whiff of black gold can also be smelled in more recent phases of Azerbaijani football. Both under the USSR and since independence, state oil institutions have played a role that can only be described as vital in the survival and development of the beautiful game. The contribution of the state oil company has grown, particularly after the country regained its independence. During the first Azerbaijan championship organised by the AFFA in 1992, institutions within the state oil company sponsored several other teams in addition to Neftchi, the quintessential oil team. The Azərneftyag oil refinery, one of SOCAR's main production sites, is the official sponsor of Neftchi; despite the fact that the refinery went out of business in 2018 and is due for demolition, the team still receives funding. SOCAR has been the main sponsor of the Azerbaijan Football Federation since 2003.

SOCAR's main commitments to the growth of football in Azerbaijan have been and still are the renovation of its dilapidated infrastructure, the improvement of services for national teams at all levels and the allocation of funds to support club teams. The Dalga, Bakcell and Bayil arenas, following oil company interventions, have hosted major sporting events, such as the first European Games in 2015, the women's Under-17 World Cup in 2012 and the men's version in 2016, and the fourth Islamic Solidarity Games in 2017. As mentioned above, the Olympic Stadium in Baku hosted the all-English Europa League Final between Chelsea and Arsenal in 2019. It also played host to half of the games in Group A – the other half were played in Rome – as well as a quarter-final of the European Championship originally scheduled for 2020 but postponed to the summer of 2021 due to the Covid pandemic.

'SOCAR does not finance Qarabag FK,' Murat Heydarov, one of the top managers at the state oil company and an AFFA executive, explains to me. 'It is an independent professional club, sponsored by one of the most important private companies in Azerbaijan. As far as we're concerned, we provide moral and emotional support for Qarabag. Unlike in other parts of Europe, in our country there are no marked differences between the fans of the various clubs, where international matches are concerned. As soon as any team starts representing Azerbaijan abroad in a UEFA competition, our population put aside their personal affiliations and commit to supporting that club on the continental stage. This is why the Azerbaijan flag can be seen flying in the stadium whenever one of our teams is involved in a game against a team from another country.'

In contrast to the achievements of Qarabag, the Azerbaijan domestic championship is experiencing a difficult period: club bankruptcies are unfortunately the order of the day and the 2017/18 Topaz Premyer Liqası season (named after its main sponsor) saw the involvement of only eight teams.

* * *

22 November 2017
Offices of Neftchi PFC
64, Nobel Avenue

'There's relatively little investment in Azerbaijani football,' explains Orkhan Huseynzade, president of

Neftchi, during the interview he kindly grants me at the headquarters of the illustrious club. 'We find it very hard to get sponsorship. We do have an institutional sponsor, but the funds it makes available to us are not enough, so we have to look for other companies willing to invest. The biggest difficulty comes from the fact that football is not that popular a sport here, or at least the domestic league isn't, given that the European cup games achieve significant audience figures.'

As I transcribe Huseynadze's words, I am reminded of what the taxi driver taking me and Arthur back to central Baku from the Olympic Stadium after Qarabag's defeat to Chelsea told us, 'Football is not a sport for Azerbaijanis,' as if to justify the heavy loss inflicted on Gurbanov's team.

'What we have to do,' continues Huseynadze, 'is commit ourselves to making football more interesting and appealing to fans over the long term. We have to work to bring them into our stadiums in ever greater numbers. It will take at least another three or four years to reach our goal, maybe more, but our national side has to qualify for the 2020 European Championship. That way we'll have the opportunity to attract more spectators to our stadiums. At the moment, football here doesn't make any profit. We only spend the sponsor's money, that's it.'

'But there has been a growth in the whole movement in recent years,' I point out.

'We have made progress over the past seven or eight years. The government decided to invest a great deal in football and we've seen the results, especially in the importance of the competitions we've been able to host. There's also a lot of attention from institutions towards the national side. But the problem with our football is the quality of the players. That's what it all comes down to. What's more, players coming from abroad stipulate in their contracts that they want to be paid in US dollars and the crisis in our local manat currency, which lost about 50 per cent of its value in 2017, certainly hasn't helped our clubs.'

There is another problem linked to Azerbaijani footballers, who choose to play abroad in far fewer numbers than their colleagues from nations of similar footballing standards, thereby missing out on the opportunity to gain international experience, useful to helping put the entire sport on an upward trajectory.

'Obviously, in situations such as Azerbaijan's, the biggest income for club teams usually comes from the export of players. But the problem is that a player who earns €100 here earns no more than €50 abroad, so our players aren't encouraged to go off to other leagues to make their fortunes. What's more, they tend not to find their feet abroad, due to problems related to the language, different lifestyle, lack of friends, etc. They find it hard to adapt. It's a complicated process. The only hope we have to raise the level of our national team is that our players will start playing in stronger leagues, even in Italy's Serie B or Germany's Zweite Bundesliga,' said Orkhan Huseynzade.

* * *

Born 53 years ago in Nakhchivan, like former president Heydar Aliyev, Rovnag Abdullayev is president of both SOCAR and the AFFA, clearly signalling how much strategic importance is placed on football by the governmental establishment of the Republic of Azerbaijan. Abdullayev has agreed to answer some questions exclusively for this book. Here is my 2017 interview with him.

How did the cooperation between SOCAR and football in Azerbaijan come about? Yours is not traditionally a country in which football is important, so why did you choose to invest in the sport?

As the state oil company of Azerbaijan, SOCAR is not only dedicated to the production and export of energy locally and internationally, but strives to contribute to the development and prosperity of our country. We believe that football is an important activity for young people across the country, especially in provincial towns and villages. As for the history of football, the first match was played in Azerbaijan more than 100 years ago and in 2011 we celebrated the 100th anniversary of Azerbaijani football with the participation of FIFA and UEFA, as well as the heads of a number of football associations from other countries. Based on an independent investigation we conducted with the help of UEFA, we discovered that football is currently the most popular sport in Azerbaijan, so we want to develop it for the enjoyment of our citizens.

Baku 2020 offers a great opportunity to broadcast the image of Azerbaijan across Europe. How have the AFFA and SOCAR invested and worked on this project?

Azerbaijan is becoming a real hub for sport. The country is located in a strategic position, at the meeting point between Asia and Europe and several other regions, such as eastern and western Europe and the Middle East and Europe. People from lots of different countries and cultures feel comfortable in our country and our people are welcoming.

With our culture of hospitality, we've demonstrated an excellent ability for organisation and have promoted ourselves seriously as a sporting hub. Both the FIFA Under-17 Women's World Cup and the UEFA European Under-17 Championship finals were staged successfully in Baku in 2012 and 2016 respectively. We're proud that Baku has been selected alongside London, Munich, Saint Petersburg and eight other cities to host the 2020 European Championship. SOCAR has shown maximum support for the AFFA initiative and acted as a guarantor together with other government organisations. We will also host the 2019 UEFA Europa League Final in Baku.

You're a major sponsor of UEFA: could the reform of the qualifying structure for the European Championship, with the Nations League, represent a real chance for Azerbaijan to take part in Baku 2020?

Obviously, the decision to create the UEFA Nations League provides another opportunity to qualify for the 2020 European Football Championship, not only for the Azerbaijani national team, but also for other nations that are at a similar level as us in terms of ranking and quality of play. Our national side will try to take advantage of this opportunity to qualify for the 2020 European Championship.

Qarabag. How do you explain the success achieved by the club from Agdam?

FK Qarabag is a very special club in Azerbaijan. It represents the Agdam region, which has been occupied by Armenian forces since 1993. The population of Agdam, together with Azerbaijani citizens from the surrounding regions, were forced by Armenian soldiers to leave their homes. The families from Agdam are currently settled in Baku until their land is liberated and they can return home. This is one of the rare cases in which a football team competing in the UEFA Champions League does not play in its home city. FK Qarabag, as a representative of the refugees, enjoys the special support of all Azerbaijani citizens and this contributes to the team's success.

Our company is particularly happy to support them. The AFFA has made a significant contribution to the team's long-term development strategy and Qarabag's success is a clear example of this: FK Qarabag have been regular participants in the group stages of UEFA club tournaments since 2013. By qualifying for the UEFA Champions League group stage, FK Qarabag have shown that Azerbaijan has great potential in football and that we can thrive even in an extremely difficult situation.

As AFFA president, the problem of money, as well as the manat crisis, is hitting Azerbaijani football hard. There are only eight teams in the top tier, some on the verge of defaulting. Is there a risk that the Premier League will become a sort of round robin? And, in the short or medium term, could it become a problem

Bottles of old USSR vodka and Azerbaijan wine and Agdam white port, circa 1980

General view of the town of Agdam which was destroyed by Armenian forces during the First Nagorno-Karabakh War. The town and its surrounding district were returned to Azerbaijani control as part of an agreement that ended the 2020 Nagorno-Karabakh War.

Rashad Sadygov, Qarabag legend

Supporters of Qarabag cheer for their team during the UEFA Champions League match in Rome

Copenhagen, Denmark. 23 August 2017. The players from Qarabag FK are in the Champions League and can here celebrate after the away Champions League qualification match against FC Copenhagen in Telia Parken

Juma Mosque in Agdam

An old picture of former Azerbaijani president Heydar Aliyev lying around in the village of Quzanli, Agdam district

Qarabag fans celebrate after the UEFA Champions League play-off second leg match against FC Copenhagen in Baku, 24 August 2017

*Maksim
Medvedev
(Qarabag),
Firenze 2016*

Azerbaijani servicemen walking through ruined buildings in the town of Agdam

Qarabag coach Gurban Gurbanov's press conference in Baku on the eve of the UEFA Champions League match versus AS Roma.

Qarabag's Miguel Michel (left) and Chelsea's N'Golo Kante (right) battle for the ball

Shusha, Divankhana square, inside the fortress walls of the Karabakh khan's palace in the beginning of the 19th century. Sovietic postcard.

Qara Qarayev (Qarabag), who started playing football in a refugee camp near Baku

Baku Olympic Stadium during the UEFA Euro 2020 Championship

Qarabag players and staff celebrate after the final whistle during the UEFA Europa Conference League 2021/22 play-off, second leg match at Pittodrie Stadium, Aberdeen.

for Qarabag, who won't have a competitive league to prepare them for big European competitions?

Adequate competition is indeed an issue we think about frequently. However, unnaturally increasing the number of teams would not have a positive impact on the development of football. This process must happen naturally. A club committed to playing in the league must firstly adhere to UEFA licensing rules and act in accordance with them. Of course, an eight-team league may not create adequate competition. But at the same time, there's also a paradoxical element. Qarabag qualified for the group stage of the Champions League having won the eight-team league for the third consecutive year. When 16, 12 and ten clubs took part in the Azerbaijani league, no clubs achieved those kinds of results. This is one of the pleasant surprises that football has given us. Let's not forget that when comparing quality and quantity in the Top League, quality should prevail. This is why our executive committee has agreed to the eight-team system.

Could Gurbanov's appointment as head coach of the Azerbaijan national team mean that Qarabag will itself increasingly become a kind of national team?

Of course, Qarabag has become the leading club in Azerbaijani football in recent years. However, this does not mean that other clubs will not be given attention when the national team is picked.

Even before the appointment of Gurban Gurbanov as national team manager, most of the side's players came from FK Qarabag.

How do you explain the choice of Gurbanov? Can you tell me exactly how this came about? Your initial thoughts, meetings with him, the decision.

Gurban Gurbanov is an Azerbaijani citizen who has gained experience in Azerbaijani football and is the top scorer in the history of the country's national side. In recent years, his experience as a manager has developed. We thought it was time to appoint a domestic professional to manage our national team, after two consecutive foreign coaches, Berti Vogts and Robert Prosinečki.

Gurbanov is a complete break with the past, with Berti Vogts and Prosinečki. Why this big change?

Berti Vogts and Robert Prosinečki were professionals with a personal philosophy who worked effectively with the Azerbaijani national team. At the same time, we've been working on the growth of our own managers, training them to UEFA standards through the relevant coach licensing system and other programmes. Right now, Gurbanov is one of our most successful coaches. We're delighted with his appointment, both professionally and for the opportunity to improve our own professional managers.

What have you asked of Gurbanov? What are his targets? And what is Gurbanov's objective with the Azerbaijan national team?

The main goal for the Azerbaijan national team is currently to qualify for the 2020 European Championship. As you know, four of the tournament's games will be played at the Baku Olympic Stadium. We all hope that our national team will have the opportunity to play in Baku in front of their home fans.

Do you think Gurbanov could become like Lobanovskyi, with a dual job for both Azerbaijan and Qarabag?

If Gurban Gurbanov has the resources to work with both teams, we have no reason to object. There's no need to compare him to Lobanovskyi or any other manager. Every manager is unique and incomparable.

Is the problem that Azerbaijani players refuse to play abroad?

We've seen this problem in Azerbaijani football for many years and the phenomenon is caused by a variety of factors. I'm sure Italians can understand that our young people love their country! However, this trend is changing and our players have gradually started playing for foreign clubs. It's probably due to the fact that their professional preparation has improved and they're much more focused on training. Nevertheless, it is still preferable to stay in your own country and have the opportunity to play than to go abroad and end up sitting on the bench.

As president, what's your personal goal for Azerbaijani football?

As president of the AFFA, I follow the GROW 2020 strategy approved by our association. That means I continue to focus on the development of grassroots of football in Azerbaijan, particularly in the regions outside the capital and in rural areas, and on the success of our national and club teams at all levels. I also hope that the participation of women in football will continue to rise in Azerbaijan.

16

Karabatsi and Qarabag

WHEN DEALING with as complex a story and as delicate an issue as war, it is important, indeed fundamental as I see it, to try to listen to both sides and report the points of view of all parties involved in the conflict. With this in mind, I tried contacting numerous journalists, politicians and professional athletes from the self-proclaimed Nagorno-Karabakh Republic or Artsakh. Unfortunately, they refused to respond once they read the questions I intended to ask them.

Saro Saryan, a veteran of the Nagorno-Karabakh war, offered to help me find contacts in Artsakh who would be prepared to answer my questions. When I showed him what I wanted to ask, he said, 'Oh! Now I understand why you can't find anyone to answer. These are provocative questions. They're divorced from how things really are so it doesn't seem logical to continue talking about them.'

But to say that everyone refused to answer wouldn't be entirely correct. The only person who read my questions and promptly replied was Hayk Khanumyan. Born on

12 September 1984 in the village of Khashtarak, in Armenia's Ijevan province, journalist Khanumyan has been president of the party he helped found in Artsakh, National Renaissance, since 1993. On 3 May 2015, he was elected to represent the party as a deputy in the National Assembly of the Nagorno-Karabakh Republic. He is also the leader of the parliamentary faction known as Renaissance, inspired by social democracy.

You changed the name of your self-proclaimed Nagorno-Karabakh Republic to the Republic of Artsakh with the constitutional referendum of 20 February. What prompted this decision?
The names Artsakh and the Nagorno-Karabakh Republic are identical in the previous and current constitution. No one has changed anything. Karabakh and Artsakh are the same names and both are commonly used.

Armenian politicians have often declared Artsakh part of Armenia. Would you give up your declared independence to join the Republic of Armenia?
The movement for Karabakh was born 30 years ago with the request to join Armenia. Artsakh was part of the ancient kingdoms of Armenia and has always been part of Armenian culture. Aspirations to reunite with the Republic of Armenia are widespread in both Artsakh and Armenia.

Do you feel Armenian or Karabatsi?
When you talk about nationality, first and foremost it's about ethnic origin, not citizenship. In this respect, most

of the people in Artsakh are Armenian. If we take into account the fact that the residents of this country have passports from the Republic of Armenia, they are also Armenians.

* * *

Pietro Kuciukian wrote in *Giardino di tenebra. Viaggio in Nagorno Karabakh*, 'We arrive in Agdam. From here, the Azeri attacked the Armenian villages. If Agdam is the symbol of the Armenian victory, it is also a secret shame, a scourge for liberated Karabakh. An entire city razed to the ground, coldly, systematically, almost patiently. If it were repopulated, which is unlikely even if peace were sealed, it would be a continuing threat to Karabakh, not dissimilar to the way the Golan Heights is to Israel.'

* * *

Pietro Kuciukian, an Armenian writer with Italian nationality, said in his book *Giardino di tenebra. Viaggio in Nagorno Karabakh* that Agdam is an ugly page in Armenian history, something that should be forgotten as soon as possible. What are your thoughts about the total destruction of the city?
Immediately after the war, both Stepanakert and Agdam were devastated. After the war, the residents of Stepanakert and other Artsakh settlements dismantled building materials from Agdam and other sites to rebuild their homes. At the time, Armenia and Artsakh were under embargo and there was a widespread shortage of many goods. Allow me to remind you that during the war, 45 per cent of Soviet Karabakh was under Azerbaijani

control for some time and many towns and villages were completely destroyed. Only 1,500 civilians were killed in the uncharacteristic bombing of Stepanakert, following shootings and attacks. This is equal to one per cent of the population of Artsakh. Consequently, the destruction of Agdam is a consequence of the war, and the war is a consequence of aggression on the part of Azerbaijan.

In 2010, you decided to wipe Agdam completely from the map by changing its name to Akna. Why did you do that? As a kind of *damnatio memoriae*?
The names of settlements change over time. In the Soviet period, there were cities across the Soviet Union that bore the names of leading Communist figures, such as Kirov, Lenin and Stepan Shaumian. After the collapse of the USSR, their names were changed almost everywhere. For example, the name of the village of Shahumyan, which is under the control of Azerbaijan, has also changed. We've changed our own names, not just Agdam, but also Lachin, Kalbajar and other places.

Do you consider Agdam part of your state? Even if it wasn't historically part of Artsakh?
Yes, Agdam is part of Artsakh. It is now and it was historically part of Artsakh. When we talk about historical Artsakh, we understand it to mean the Meliks of Armenian Khamsa, which existed between the 15th and 18th centuries, as well as in the early Middle Ages. Even before that there was a state of Artsakh that was part of the Armenian kingdoms.

Qarabag Agdam FK, known as the team without a home or from the ghost city, are doing well in Europe. What's your opinion on that?

The idea of a club in exile is an interesting one. You Italians could create a football team called Tripoli and have them compete in the European Champions League, because the Libyan city was once part of your state. In the same way, France could create a club called Algiers, Germany one called Gdansk. Something similar also exists among Armenians: for example, there are districts of Yerevan named after cities in Armenia that we've lost and are now under the control of Turkey, such as Marash, Malatia, Sebastia and others.

What do you think of a club with the name Agdam, given that you consider the city yours?

I don't see the problem. When it comes to football, I'm interested in the game, not the names.

The narrative around Qarabag uses the Agdam argument a lot to motivate the players, to set goals and tell them that one day they'll be able to play back in the city again. Do you think that could ever really happen?

It's obvious that the Azerbaijanis would not have lost Agdam and other cities if they hadn't resorted to aggression against the people of Artsakh. I think Azerbaijan would lose more territories in the event of renewed aggression. The only way they can return to Agdam, part of Artsakh, is to seek peace and live in peace. There is no other way.

I'm going to say something provocative now: why don't you give Agdam back to Azerbaijan and try to keep the old territory of the Nagorno-Karabakh Oblast under your control?

Have you ever heard that Azerbaijan is ready to recognise the independence of Artsakh in exchange for anything? There's no solution to the Karabakh problem that includes territorial concessions. After all, the question came up when Agdam and the other regions were not part of Artsakh, so it isn't a question of territories, but something completely different. Azerbaijan wants to destroy Armenians from Artsakh who live within Artsakh's borders. The president of Azerbaijan talks about taking over Yerevan and other parts of Armenia as well.

Is peace still possible?

It is possible, but not now. The perspectives of the parties involved in the conflict are too far apart at the moment. I think peace will confirm the de facto borders that exist today.

Why does Armenia not recognise Artsakh or the Nagorno-Karabakh Republic? Perhaps because yours is a puppet state that Armenia is just waiting for the right moment to annex so it can construct Greater Armenia?

Greater Armenia existed as a kingdom at the beginning of the Middle Ages over an area of 300,000 square kilometres. Together, modern-day Armenia and Artsakh measure approximately 42,000 square kilometres. Consequently, it would not be possible to create Greater Armenia by annexing Artsakh. I think it's wrong to deny that Artsakh is part of Armenia. If Armenia recognised Artsakh, the international process of recognition would be accelerated. But Armenia doesn't want to do this so it doesn't damage the negotiation process within the OSCE framework.

Are you planning to join UEFA as Artsakh?
You have to have a domestic championship in order to join UEFA and that doesn't exist in Artsakh.

Are there any Qarabag fans in Artsakh?
I don't know, I haven't come across any sociological surveys on football preferences.

Ter-Petrosyan has said that returning Agdam and the regions not part of historical Nagorno-Karabakh might be a good solution to the conflict. Why don't you take the words of the wise former president of Armenia into consideration?
Do you mean the areas not included in Karabakh in Soviet times? As I've already said, historical Artsakh is a different concept and all the territories that are now part of the Republic of Artsakh were part of it. President Ter-Petrosyan resigned from office in 1998 because of this position. He stood in the Armenian parliamentary elections with the same manifesto a year ago and won just two per cent of the total votes. People who hold that opinion are marginal in Armenia. Of course, I don't agree with this opinion and I believe that any territorial transfer should be out of the question. Furthermore, any territorial concessions will cause a new war and endanger the inhabitants of Artsakh.

17

The future of Qarabag

24 November 2017
Azersun Arena, Surakhani, Baku

The suburb of Surakhani, about 25km from the centre of Baku, is known for the Fire Temple, a monastic complex that encompasses a Zoroastrian place of worship. Built over a natural gas field, in ancient times its gas emissions would catch fire, creating flames thought by believers to be inextinguishable. As a result, Azerbaijan is known as the 'Land of Fire', a nickname that appeared on Atlético Madrid's strip from 2013 to 2015 in a sponsorship deal that was not without controversy. There was much discussion in Spain as to whether the slogan of a country whose president Ilham Aliyev has been accused of violating human rights at home, concerning freedom of the press in particular, should have been given such exposure.

Since June 2015, Surakhani has also been home to the newly built headquarters of Qarabag FK, constructed on the back of major investment from Azersun Holding. The aim was to provide the team from Agdam, in forced exile since 1993, with a ground at which to train and a venue for their home games. The complex also plays host to the Azersun Arena, a modern 5,800-seater stadium often used by Qarabag for Azerbaijani league games. The stadium is closed on three sides, open only on one of its long sides, which overlooks the club's training ground.

As the sun sets in Surakhani, Gurban Gurbanov is running down the sideline in the company of his faithful lieutenant Rashad Sadigov, at the end of a training session for all those who did not take to the pitch against Chelsea the previous night. Team captain Sadigov, who received a red card after less than 20 minutes of the game, is duly present, perhaps to let off steam or more likely to set an example to the younger players. To convey the spirit of Qarabag Agdam, to show them how, even in the face of the bitterest defeats and humiliations, you have to keep your head down and work hard, ready for the next challenge. Ready to prove your worth and pride.

Gurbanov leaves Sadigov, who heads into the middle of the pitch to carry out some drills with his team-mates, and walks towards me. I'm waiting for him alongside Arthur and Nurlan, the club's press officer who will interpret from Azerbaijani into English for the chat that the Qarabag manager and the new manager of the Azerbaijan side has agreed to have with us.

The initials QG (read as GG in Azerbaijani) stand out on his blue sweatshirt; his face is that of a boxer, while his eyes reveal character and charisma in spades. The first time we were in touch was in September 2017 when he agreed to grant me an interview, via email, for the Indian sport website Sportskeeda, which I used to write for occasionally.

In that interview, he prophetically declared that Roma were on a par with Atlético Madrid and Chelsea when most pundits had dismissed their chances of finishing any higher than third in their Champions League group. Back then, I was particularly struck by the final sentence he added at the end of one of his answers, 'Also, I see that you got enough information about Azerbaijan and our occupied territories. Thank you for this.'

We then met in person during the pre-match press conference before Qarabag-Chelsea, at which he greeted me publicly before answering a question from a local reporter; we also shook hands at the end. From the training ground bench at the Qarabag-owned facility next to the Azersun Arena, he listens to the questions interpreted by Nurlan, his eyes constantly studying the movements of his players as they go through the final part of their training session. At first glance, it looks as if he's distracted, but he pays close attention to the questions asked and measures his responses carefully.

How do you feel the day after losing to Chelsea?
We're disappointed, saddened by last night's result. Everyone knows how good Chelsea are. I'm disappointed because we didn't get the chance to play our best football, our best possible match in what was a sold-out stadium. The fans only got to see 20 minutes of a proper game.

When Rashad received the red card, did you have to change the tactics you'd prepared after just 20 minutes?
We'd all prepared very thoroughly for the game. All the players, the whole team really wanted it. We were really

motivated to give it our best shot. That wasn't part of our plan, of course. It never crossed our minds that we would have to handle a situation like that. We were ready for any eventuality, any kind of action on the pitch, but not to be on the receiving end of a red card just 20 minutes in. I'm not clear on the reason for the red card. Chelsea didn't need a sending-off, a penalty or to play against ten men for 70 minutes. It's not about the result.

As the manager of a small club, it seems as if decisions like that always go in favour of the big teams. As a citizen of Azerbaijan, the homeland of freedom and rights, I wonder whether a decision like that, an attitude like that, is right. Football is a contact sport, but this was a cruel decision. We might have lost the game anyway, but that decision was the most incredible I've seen during my entire career. But when things like that happen, they help us grow, to make us stronger. We've got to learn from these situations, to keep our cool when things like that happen.

When Rashad was sent off, the whole team, except the keeper Šehić, gathered around you near the sideline. What did you say to them?

I saw that their heads had gone down, that they were slumping, so I called them over. They were devastated. I tried to motivate them, to encourage them and assign them specific tasks. I had to make decisions, but I told them to never give up.

Can you explain the importance of Rashad to you personally and to the team as a whole?

Everyone knows we're friends, but he's a friend to all our players. As a leader he always sets an example to the other players, who follow what he does on the pitch and what he tells them, as they do with me. Not only that; how he behaves on the pitch, how he leads the team, is very important to me too! Not only for Qarabag but also for the Azerbaijan national side. If the team needs to be calmed down, he calms them down; if they need to be motivated, he motivates them. He always knows what the right decision is for the team, for his team-mates on the pitch. Every manager would love to have a captain like Rashad on their team. He can finish off what I'm thinking and conveys my ideas on to the pitch.

You became friends at Neftchi, didn't you?
Yes, when we were both playing there.

Can you tell us how you started out in football?
I was born in Zaqatala. I came to football late. My older brother Moussa introduced me to the sport. I started playing when I was 15, but I worked hard, really hard and followed in my brother's footsteps. Before I discovered football I was interested in sports in general. I was very active and I liked all sports. It didn't take me long to get into the first team, though, because I was physically more ready than my peers and within four years I started playing for the national team. I earned my first cap at 18. But I have to admit that I worked too hard during those years. I'm like that not just when it comes to football, but in every aspect of my life. If I want something, if I'm interested in something, I give everything to get it. I

work hard to achieve my objectives. Thank God. God has helped me reach my goals through hard work.

When you were at Daşqın Zaqatala, your first club in the USSR league, did you ever play in Agdam?
I remember the Imaret Stadium. I remember their fans talking too much, shouting and singing. They were a tough side to play against. The pitch was great and the stadium was also really nice. I remember a game in 1992/93, when the war had already started. A bomb came down suddenly while we were playing. I remember the sound really clearly.

When did you decide to become a manager?
I was playing abroad in Russia. I was about 30 and I started taking notes from my manager and becoming more interested in the job.

When you came to Qarabag in 2009, you inherited a team of foreigners. What decisions did you make? With the exception of Admir Teli, you built a team of just Azerbaijani players. Was that your decision or the club's? What was the idea behind that choice?
The idea was to renew the team, to regenerate it. That was my first objective. I wanted local footballers to be able to play more and win more. There were plenty of interesting prospects, really talented players. Players who didn't have the chance to play before I arrived, but were really talented. I gave them the chance to show what they could do in Europe, to play their football, to show what they were capable of on the big stage. Maybe it was a risk,

but it's been successful. My second objective was to create a winning team in the shortest possible time.

Rashad Sadigov and Aslan Kerimov were the two experienced players in that team, two leaders. How did that come about?

I played with them both at Neftchi, but they had two different styles of leadership. Aslan was the captain, signed from Turkey to play in Europe. Having as many players as possible like that is every manager's dream. There was no need to set down any rules, because they led the team.

Step by step you and Qarabag have scaled greater and greater heights. Firstly, the Azerbaijan title, then the Europa League play-offs, qualification for the groups and now the Champions League group stage. What's your secret?

You have to take your time; you have to constantly repeat your goals to yourself and the team. It takes time, but the more you repeat and insist on the concepts you believe in, you'll succeed. My philosophy is not to look at what I have done, but at what I haven't done. Looking back, I look at my mistakes and try to correct them. You can be successful if you learn from the mistakes you've made.

You're always keen to learn from the greats. Who are your role models? Who are you inspired by?

To be honest, I'm more interested in the philosophy of a team than in the manager. More in the philosophy than the person. I'm interested in all the mindsets and styles that are similar to ours, which can be adapted and replicated in Azerbaijan with the players I have at my disposal. As a philosophy, when I was at Barcelona, where I spent a week in contact with all the teams, all the different ages, I saw how you play clean, intelligent football. I use these methods more than others. That doesn't mean I only use Barça's methods, but I think their methods and system provide the greatest benefits in modern football. But football changes day by day. There are new questions, new commitments and you have to be constantly studying, always looking for new ideas and solutions. However, in the end, it all comes down to being good with the ball!

One of the things you believe in most is possession.
The idea is that the longer you keep the ball, the more chance you have of scoring. Added to that, your opponents can't score. Sometimes you do have to adapt to the other team's game though, and scoring with a long ball can be easier, as it sometimes was with Reynaldo.

You've recently become the coach of the Azerbaijani national team. With the new Nations League structure, how do you see your chances of qualifying for Euro 2020? Will you keep up both roles for the national side and for the club?
I will carry on managing Qarabag, God willing! I think every team in our Nations League group has a good chance of qualifying. Everyone thinks they have an opportunity to make it to the finals.

Theoretically, Azerbaijan could have to play Armenia in the Nations League, something that's been made impossible in recent years by international organisations. What do you think?

Yes, we could have to face each other in the final. And if it did happen, it would be at a neutral ground, behind closed doors. But I hope we never have to meet the enemy.

Azerbaijan's Top League is seeing fewer and fewer teams at the start of each season. The system is losing teams while Qarabag are getting stronger and stronger. Do you think there's a risk of it becoming a one-club league? And what might the consequences for the national side be?

These problems are linked to inflation in the manat. We have to grow our football, our system. Everyone has to think about their own club, commit to giving their best and work hard without thinking about the other teams or the fact that there are eight teams. We always have to give our best to get the best results. The top-tier teams in Europe are 30 or 40 years ahead of us. I don't think I'm exaggerating, even if we have qualified for the Champions League. We still have lots of growing to do.

You said a little while ago that what matters are philosophy, mindset and continuously repeating the concepts a manager wants to pursue until they get into the minds of their players. Are they inspired by being a team from Agdam? I see it repeated over and over again; even the new players understand that their team isn't from Baku, but comes from and belongs to

another city. Does this help you in your work and with team spirit?

You're absolutely right! Even the newest players, when they arrive, they're given information about the situation immediately. But they also get information about where they're going before they get here. Players who sign for Qarabag are immediately made aware. We want to tell them the truth, the facts as they are, without exaggerating. We want to make them understand the true meaning of this team, which is completely different to the clubs they come from, and to make them understand that Qarabag is first and foremost a family.

Do you think you'll get to play in Agdam again one day or is that just a dream?

We live with this hope constantly. We know that our government is focused on this as its main goal. The government's efforts are ongoing and I believe that one day we'll have the chance to play in our city again. Maybe I won't be here anymore by then, but I believe that one day a Qarabag manager and team will make our dream come true. It won't be easy, not least because it's an objective that doesn't depend on us. There are too many decisions in the hands of others. We did play for a while in Guzanli, but the stadium in Guzanli is not the Imaret. I know it well, having played there as an opponent.

Do you feel like the manager of a team from Agdam, even if your new ground is just outside the capital?

Of course, we represent Agdam and Karabakh.

* * *

'The club hasn't given us a clear objective for next season, about where we need to get to in the next Champions League,' Ansi Agolli tells me straight after mathematically securing the sixth, and fifth consecutive, domestic title in the history of Qarabag. 'We'll see what happens. It's going to be tough to repeat the emotions of the past season with the whole of Azerbaijan celebrating our journey in the competition. We'll play, prepare for every game and see what football has in store for us.'

The only certainty about the future is that Qarabag will continue to represent Karabakh, its land and its people, refugees, displaced people, those who have lost their homes, jobs, schools and seen relatives and friends die in a fratricidal war of unprecedented violence. Qarabag will continue to bring a story of suffering and exile to the football pitches of Europe, but also one of great achievements, representing the redemption of an entire people and an entire nation.

Qarabag is Agdam; Qarabag is Azerbaijan.

Afterword

Return to Agdam

IT TOOK a war, another one, for Agdam to regain the place it had been given on the map, before it was snatched away by weapons. I will use these lines to attempt to reconstruct what happened on 27 September 2020, when a new conflict broke out in the region known as Nagorno-Karabakh. Who opened the hostilities has never been made clear, but for six weeks the armies of the self-proclaimed Republic of Artsakh and Azerbaijan fought for possession of the disputed region and provinces.

I have written several times that the Bishkek agreements were not a real peace treaty and that the crux of a situation left, to some extent voluntarily, unresolved and ambiguous, would eventually come under scrutiny. And that was exactly what happened. But, compared to the conflict of the early 1990s, the values on the ground have since been reversed; Aliyev's army, supported militarily by Turkey, is decidedly stronger than the army financed and supported by Armenia, which is in full economic and political crisis, with premier Nikol Pashinyan increasingly challenged by public opinion.

The conflict came to an end with a ceasefire agreement signed on 9 November 2020 by the president of Azerbaijan, the prime minister of Armenia and the president of the Russian Federation Vladimir Putin, ending all hostilities in the region. The president of the self-proclaimed Republic of Artsakh, Arayik Harutyunyan, also agreed to put an end to the fighting. The agreement signed by all the warring parties provides, in addition to the end of hostilities and the presence of a Russian peacekeeping contingent for five years to ensure compliance with the provisions, the return of historically important cities such as Shusha to Azerbaijani control. The blue, red and green flag with the crescent moon and eight-pointed star will fly over the ruins of Agdam once more.

And so it was that, on 28 November 2020, the whole Qarabag team, led by the club's directors, was able to return to visit the ruins of the Imaret Stadium, 27 years after the last match played in their city. 'We are home!' read the post on the club's official Facebook page. The end of a nightmare, the return home.

The beginning of a new story.

Acknowledgements

THE FIRST person I feel I should thank after writing this book is my wife Veronica, who encouraged and supported me (as well as put up with me) at every stage of the process, from researching the material, travelling and the writing itself. Without forgetting my daughter Adele Rosa, my son Leonida and Niccolò. My brother Daniele for his crucial help.

Then there are my fellow adventurers on the journey I set out on in Baku. I'm referring first and foremost to Rustam Fataliyev and Arthur Huizinga, whom you have already met. Our working relationship has developed into a firm friendship that goes beyond our national borders and has seen us create a WhatsApp group with the emblematic and self-deprecating name 'No World Cup for Us', with the three flags of Azerbaijan, Italy and Holland. Other people whom I got to know personally in the Azerbaijani capital and deserve thanks include the great Thomas Goltz, who assigned me the honour of writing the third part of the story of Qarabag (after his own and that of Arthur), Shakir Eminbeyli and Azhdars, Rustam's friend.

A special mention goes to Nurlan Ibrahimov, former head of the press office at Qarabag Agdam FK and, alongside him, other members of the club who have contributed, in many different ways, to this book: Elvar Guliyev, Yusuf Huseyn, Gurban Gurbanov, Ansi Agolli, Richard Almeida, Shahid Hasanov, Mushfiq Huseynov, Yashar Huseynov, Elshad Khudadatov, Emrah Celikel, Dani Quintana and Asif Asgarov. Among the club's former players, Sattar Aliyev, Giorgi Adamia, Muarem Muarem, Aron-Arif Zarbailov and Anatoli Ponomarev are worthy of mention.

In the hope that I have not forgotten anyone, I would also like to thank Gadar Hasanov, son of Shadid Hasanov, who works for rivals Neftchi, but was instrumental in organising and translating the interview with his father; Giovanni Melchiorre, the Italian fitness trainer currently at Kayserispor, who spent long spells with Neftchi and Khazar Lankaran; the ambassadors Augusto Massari and Mammad Ahmadzada, and the latter's press secretary, Barbara Cassani; Mario Raffaelli, current president of Amref Italia and former president of the peace conference for Nagorno-Karabakh; the writer Vahid Qazi; the journalists Marut Vanian, Ayaz Mirzayev, Elsever Memmedov, Kenan Mastaliyev, Asaf Quliyev, Stefano Fonsato, Damiano Benzoni and Manu Veth; the guys from the Imaret Fan Club: Elvin Asadov, Elvin Ibrahimov, Isko Babazade, Nato Babayev, Vusal Ahmadov, Zaur Mammadov Zakiroglu; The European Azerbaijan Society, Neil Watson, František Laurinec, Michele Uva, Jamilia Mehdiyeva, Saro Saryan, Ibrahim Zada, Elshan Alasgarov, Vusal Agamirov and Hayk Khanumyan.

Bibliography

Alex Jones, Tom Master, Virginia Maxwell, John Noble, *Lonely Planet Georgia, Armenia and Azerbaijan* (Lonely Planet, 2016)

Arthur Huizinga, *Nooit een thuiswedstrijd. Een voetbaloorlog in de Kaukasus* (Prometheus, Amsterdam, 2012)

Domenico Letizia, *Il Nagorno-Karabakh tra diritto internazionale, Corte penale internazionale e la sentenza della Corte Europea dei diritti dell'uomo del giugno 2015* (Youcanprint, 2017)

Evgeny Vinokurov, *A Theory of Enclaves* (Lexington Books, 2007)

Franco Rossi, *Perda il migliore. Il paradosso di 15 mondiali di calcio* (Limina, 1998)

Jonathan Wilson, *Behind the curtain. Travel in Eastern European Football* (Orion, London, 2006)

Marco Belinazzo, *Goal economy. Come la finanza globale ha trasformato il calcio* (Baldini + Castoldi, 2015)

Mikhail Gorbachev, *On My Country and the World* (Columbia University Press, New York, 2000)

Parag Khanna, *The Second World: Empires and Influence in the New Global Order* (Penguin, 2009)

Patrick Wilson Gore, *'Tis some poor fellow's skull, Post-Soviet Warfare in the Southern Caucasus* (iUniverse, Lincoln, 2008)

Pietro Kuciukian, *Giardino di tenebra. Viaggio in Nagorno Karabakh* (Guerini e Associati, Milan, 2017)

Steve LeVine, *The Oil and the Glory: The Pursuit of Empire and Fortune on the Caspian Sea* (Random House, New York, 2007)

Suha Bolukbasi, *Azerbaijan: A Political History* (I.B. Tauris, 2011)

The Zoryan Institute For Contemporary Armenian Research & Documentation, *The Karabagh Files*, Gerard J. Libaridian ed. (Cambridge Toronto, 1988)

Thomas de Waal, *Black Garden, Armenia and Azerbaijan Through Peace and War* (New York University Press, 2003)

Thomas Goltz, *Azerbaijan Diary: A Rogue Reporter's Adventures in an Oil-rich, War-torn, Post-Soviet Republic* (Routledge, London, 1999)

Vahid Qazi, *Ruhlar şəhəri* [City of Ghosts] (MHS, Baku, 2011)

I also consulted the archives of the following newspapers and magazines: *Il Corriere della Sera, La Stampa, La Repubblica, La Gazzetta dello Sport, Il Fatto Quotidiano, IRS-Patrimonio, Pravda, New York Times, Visions of Azerbaijan, Marca, FourFourTwo, Ultimo Uomo, Rivista Undici, The Guardian, Lenin Yolu, L'Équipe, Kavkaz, The Economist.*

The contents found on the following websites were also invaluable: Qarabag Agdam FK (www.qarabagh.

com), AFFA (www.affa.az), Vahid Qazi's blog (https://vahidqazi.wordpress.com/), The Rec Sport Soccer Statistics Foundation (www.rsssf.com), International Federation of Football History & Statistics (https://iffhs.de/), Mountainous Karabakh (http://www.mountainous-karabakh.org/), Azernews (www.azernews.az), Panarmenian (www.panarmenian.net), Eurasianet (www.eurasianet.org), Osservatorio Balcani Caucaso (www.balcanicaucaso.org), Presidenza della Repubblica dell'Azerbaigian (www.azerbaijan.az), Futbolgrad (www.futbolgrad.com), and Damiano Benzoni's Dinamo Babel blog (https://dinamobabel.wordpress.com) Eurosport (www.eurosport.it), Global Firepower, Human Rights Watch (www.hrw.org/), https://karabakh.org, Pravda.ru Sportskeeda (www.sportskeeda.com) and many more.